For Teachers With Love
Helping Educators Become Significant

Ora Zohar

with Aviva Pinchuk, Sara Wieder and Chava Zohar

Edited by Israel Sykes

ISBN: 978-1-941733-11-0

Published by EA Books, Inc.
www.eabooksonline.com

Dedication

Over three decades I directed the National Center for Staff Development at the Hebrew University in Jerusalem. My staff and I worked in Israel and around the world with thousands of educators, department chairpersons and principals.

None of this could have happened without the involvement of two extraordinary mentors who believed in me, in the Center's staff and in our proposed model. Together they made our dream possible.

In 1973, Dwight Allen, then Dean of the School of Education at the University of Massachusetts in Amherst, attended a summer course for English teachers as a guest of the Ministry of Education. He introduced participants to the model of teaching as craft across subject matter and academic level. His concept of teaching as a collection of specific skills that can be defined, identified, practiced and perfected shaped much of the Center's work with school practitioners. His demonstration of microteaching, especially the observation and feedback stages, proved helpful in countless workshops. Dwight visited twice, teaching and inspiring everyone with his passion and vibrant devotion to the educational profession.

Professor Seymour Fox, of blessed memory, Dean of the School of Education at Hebrew University in Jerusalem, heard the vision of a National Center for Staff Development and dared to take a gamble on it. He offered recognition and a home base at one of Israel's finest universities, along with his blessings and support. He funded the first two years of staff training, well before the Center could offer workshops and generate income for the University.

The combination of Dwight's theories and Seymour's practical support significantly shaped the form and character of the Center. I gratefully dedicate this book to them both.

Acknowledgments

Everyone is so excited!!! Amazing they say, At last, at last, the book is almost finished! Hurry up and finish it, all you need now are the acknowledgements…. That is very easy… Really, I say, okay if it is so easy…. I will immediately work on that…and I do…. I ask myself a basic question. After so many years of work in the field, with so many people helping, supporting, cooperating, encouraging. HOW DO I THANK THEM ALL? I think, consider, recall, and reflect and answer myself: it is IMPOSSIBLE! If I thank 100 people who really should be noted, I may forget 200 others whom we should thank and acknowledge… So, what to do?

My solution: With hearts full of gratitude, I thank colleagues and staff of the School of Education of Hebrew University of Jerusalem, and colleagues and staff of the Melton Center for Jewish Education at Hebrew University. I especially thank Alan Hoffman, Howard Dietcher, and Jonny Cohen who so generously included the Center in so many seminars they gave for overseas groups that, in fact, we ourselves came to believe that we were part of the Melton Family.

Scores of members of the Ministry of Education were staunch supporters of the Center over the years… Special thanks to the late Minister of Education Zevulun Hammer of blessed memory, to his executive director Shimshon Shoshanni, and to Avraham Ohr, national supervisor for development for schools, who made it possible for us to work with many schools in the periphery.

Many educators abroad welcomed my colleagues and me into their homes, schools and hearts. We carry many wonderful memories from these experiences and thank them all for special connections during and after our work together.

I thank all the hundreds of participants in our workshops throughout the years and throughout Israel whose written feedback warmed our hearts and gave us energy to keep up the good work.

In 1996 I spent a sabbatical semester in York University in Toronto, where I was warmly hosted by Professor Michael Connelly in OISE, the Ontario Institute for Studies in Education, who provided me with physical space. Michael affirmed for me for the first time what I knew in my heart about the place of narrative in educational research, and thanks to his coaching, I wrote the narrative at the beginning of this book. I am grateful for all his encouragement, including the testimonial for this book.

I am particularly indebted to a group of 16 principals of the Principals' Center who answered our call years ago and embarked with us upon a research process that led ultimately to this book. Thanks to Yoel Ortal, Chaim Deitchman, Aziz Daim, Tamar Wolfin, Shimon Yidgar, Dr. Zvi Yarblum, Dr. Anat Leibovitz, Dr. Shoshana Lichtenstadt, Chaya Maor, Zehava Messinger, Vered Marom, Ada Nagar, Esther Foster, Nurit Ramati, Roni Sagi, Afif Abu Ful.

I have been blessed to work with marvelous colleagues and friends throughout my professional life, some of whose voices can be found in this book. I am grateful to each one beyond measure, for their friendship and support. My exceptionally devoted colleagues Aviva Pinchuk, Sara Wieder and Chava Zohar, and my wonderful son-in-law Israel Sykes, deserve special mention for their loyalty throughout the extensive concept-to-product phase of this book.

A number of people read previous drafts of the book, and the current version reflects their important contributions. Special thanks to Iri Kessel, Dr. Saul Wachs and Dr. Sylvia Schonfeld for their close readings and helpful suggestions.

On a personal level, I am grateful to my amazing family, children and grandchildren for their encouragement and of course, above all, to my husband Yitzchak for his loving support these six decades, from urging me to accept Dwight's invitation, through the years of my travels to work in schools around the world.

I am grateful for the good fortune I have had to be deeply involved in work that I loved...thank you LIFE.

Ora Zohar, Jerusalem
September 2014

Table of Contents

Preface: Introducing Miss A

She came to the attention of Canadian educators in the late 1970s, when a study of adults who had once sat in her first grade classroom revealed some astonishing information. Eigil Pedersen, a professor in the faculty of education at McGill University in Montreal, found on examining the school records of 189 students who attended Royal Arthur School[1] in the early 1950s, that those who were lucky enough to have had Miss Apple Daisy[2] in first grade were subsequently more successful in school than those who had either of the other two first-grade teachers at Royal Arthur. At that time, it was accepted that IQ scores generally remained constant. Nevertheless, many of these children were shown by the records to have scored increasingly higher on IQ tests as their schooling progressed.

Pedersen went on to track down and interview 60 former students of the three first- grade teachers and discovered something even more amazing. When measuring status according to level of education, occupation, type of dwelling and personal appearance, he found that in Miss Apple Daisy's class, 64 percent had achieved high adult status, 36 percent had achieved medium adult status and **none** of her students had low adult status. Of the students in the other two classes, only 29 percent achieved high adult status, 33 percent achieved medium adult status and 38 percent had low adult status.

Miss Apple Daisy was obviously doing something right. But what was it? What seemingly secret method did she have of instilling self-confidence and a love of learning in her students? Interviews with former pupils and colleagues revealed some characteristics of her 34 years of teaching at Royal Arthur. She never lost her temper or resorted to physical restraint and showed obvious affection for the children. She believed it was her job to fill each child with a positive self-concept, and a belief in his or her ability to learn and achieve. She was determined that every one of her pupils would read by the end of the year, regardless of

---

[1] This is a fictional name.

[2] This was not her real name, but rather what the children called her because her real name, Lole Appugliese, was too difficult to pronounce.

background or ability. She impressed upon them the importance of schooling and why they should continue. She taught the children who were slow learners after school hours. If her pupils forgot their lunches, Miss Apple Daisy gave them some of her own. Even after 20 years, she could remember each former pupil by name.

A former pupil summarized her secret for success in this way: "How did she teach? With a lot of love!"

Introduction

Years ago, when I was co-leading a seminar in Toronto, a few participants asked: "How many years have you been teaching?"

Calculating quickly, I told them – "Fifty years."

"And your colleague?"

"About the same."

"WOW!" – They turned to the group in awe. "We're learning from 100 years of experience!"

Dear Reader,

Who are you? Where are you? Are you a teacher in a classroom? A school principal? An involved citizen? A concerned parent? A university student? If so, in writing this book, I have had you in mind.

In this Western world of the 21st century, our children, at an early age, face many years of compulsory education. As parents, we have good reason to be deeply concerned about the quality of our children's lives during those many long hours. It was out of this concern that I first became passionate about helping professional educators develop.

In 1978 I founded the National Center for Staff Development at the School of Education at the Hebrew University of Jerusalem. The work of the Center, and subsequently of our Principals' Center, was explicitly grounded on the following core convictions:

1. Every individual has a need to develop his or her own potential.

2. Development requires the presence and nurturing involvement of significant others.

3. School staff are potential significant adults in the lives of pupils.

4. The potential to be significant to others can be systematically developed.

These core convictions shaped the two foundations of our programs: a coherent curriculum and a powerfully nurturing culture. This combination created a strong training model that proved applicable in a wide variety of professional settings: with kindergarten teachers as well as university lecturers, with teachers of all specializations, throughout Israel and in countries around the world.

We helped turn countless schools into fertile ground for learning and growth. Early on, we learned that in order to facilitate growth for those who "live" in schools – children and adults, pupils and faculty – schools must provide the nurturing environment essential to growth. We believed that if school staff experienced, enjoyed and understood the deliberately crafted nurturing environments we modeled in our workshops, they would in turn bring a similar atmosphere into their own schools and classrooms. Creation of such an environment for teachers, department chairs, principals and other professionals was therefore fundamental to the Center's programs. Many who experienced the impact of the Center have testified enthusiastically to the value and contribution of this approach.

This book opens with the story of my own personal and professional journey that led to the founding of the Center, and continues with the story of the Center itself. The rest of the book shares the work of the Center, as told in many voices, over time, and in many places. The book is like a collage, a colorful warm patchwork quilt made out of stories, reflections, concepts, tools for personal and staff development, and the voices of teachers, principals, and Center staff. Each patch can be read and appreciated independently, and a glossary is provided at the end of the book to help with navigation. If read together, a cohesive clear integrated pattern will emerge that, over time, will hopefully become a part of you and your own educational practice – whether as teacher, principal, or parent.

In 2005, after nearly thirty years of generative practice, systemic changes dried up the Center's sources of funding, causing the Center to close down. Unfortunately, since we were much better at teaching and facilitating than at publishing, little of the Center's work was systematically documented, leaving its rich and multidimensional practice unavailable in written form for the next generation of teacher educators.

We have written the present book in order to make the rich history and the unique expertise and resources of the Center available to the many professionals who believe wholeheartedly that education should be a significant and meaningful experience for all involved, one that fosters human growth, community and a better society. This was the essence of the Center and this is its legacy.

Who is "We"?

Throughout the book, "we" are very active – we plan, we train teachers and we lead workshops. We travel to schools all over the country and to Jewish communities around the world. It is only natural to wonder: Who is "we?"

"We" are actually two voices: The inclusive "we" refers to the 25 teachers on the Center's staff throughout the years, as well as students and other partners. The "we" who have written this book together, is a narrower subset including Aviva Pinchuk, Sara Wieder, and Chava Zohar – veteran members of the National Center for Staff Development – and Dr. Ora Zohar. We have spent much of our professional lives together, and have written this account collaboratively in order to leave a written record of our work. The picture below catches us at one of our many meetings with Israel Sykes, our editor, in our "office" in the lobby of the Inbal Hotel in Jerusalem.

While Ora's is the primary voice – in particular the autobiographical background in chapter 1 – the book integrates a variety of voices, including staff members and graduates of the Center's programs. When a story or narrative reflects the personal experiences or thoughts of an individual, this is indicated by the specific author name.

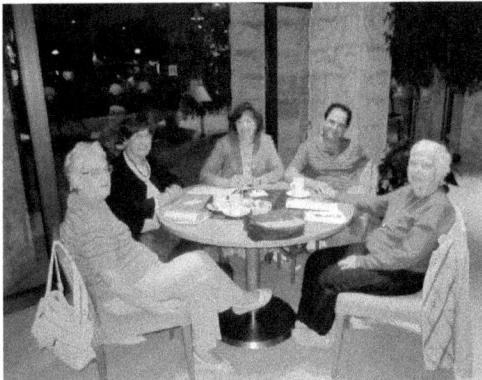

Chapter 1
Beginnings – A Personal Narrative

The passion of my professional life has been the bettering of schools. Simply, I want schools to be better than many of them are. I want schools to be places where children are happy and are helped to grow, in all the ways that we mean when talking about healthy development. I often ask myself where this passion comes from and why it is so urgent.

Hundreds of teachers and graduate students over the years have told me that they always wanted to become teachers. They remember organizing classes of neighborhood children as preschoolers, handing out crayons and paper and planning songs and games. I am impressed by the clarity of their early interest.

I remember myself as a small, sturdy child in the 1930's in P.S. 180 in Brooklyn, a neighborhood elementary school bursting with energy, laughter, and hundreds of Italian, Irish and Jewish boys and girls. I loved every day of my years in that school, as I later loved every day at Midwood High School (skipping over, however, my disastrous junior high years). While it is clear to me now that my passion is rooted in my own joyous school life and later disappointment in the less than idyllic school experience of others, still, there was no early decision to be involved in the bettering of schools. My teenage dream was to study law and join my beloved father in his law practice. With his sudden death during my senior year of high school, that plan was upset. At the same time I became a leader in a Zionist youth movement in Brooklyn – a role rooted in my family's history.

I was born in Jerusalem to American parents who had come to Israel with a personal vision of rebuilding a vibrant Jewish community in the ancient homeland of the Jewish people. My father had hoped he could establish himself as a lawyer and raise his family in Jerusalem. When this did not work out, it was with a sense of heartbreak that my parents returned to New York. They had come with three children, and returned with four —a girl of three and a half, who already realized her special identity as the *sabra*[3], born during their golden years in Jerusalem.

As a young teenager, it was natural for me to join a local Zionist youth movement, whose members were committed to going to Israel and living on *kibbutz*.[4] The local branch was an hour's walk from home. A decision was made to open a branch closer to home and I became the leader of this fledgling group. This meant planning activities that would draw local teens into the movement and hold their interest. There had to be songs, folk-dancing and a serious but lively weekly discussion. Today, I recognize that planning this weekly activity was my first experience in developing lesson plans. I took the responsibility very seriously, probably as a matter of pride, as only stimulating activities would guarantee me a return audience.

Two years later a group of us – including Yitzchak Zohar, also a member of the movement and my future husband – were sent to Guelph, Ontario, to a farm where we would learn about the *kibbutz* life style in preparation for our future in Israel. While the experience of collective life made it clear to me that *kibbutz* life was not for me, that year in Guelph opened an unexpected door into the teaching profession. There were 40 Jewish families in Guelph who saw in our arrival an opportunity for the Jewish education of their children. A delegation soon came to the farm asking us to organize Sunday school activities. This became my responsibility. Every Sunday I changed out of jeans and work boots, put on a dress and city shoes and was driven to the community building where I taught the children about Judaism.

I remember my amazement that first day, entering a large room filled with children aged six to fourteen, sensing the tremendous excitement heralding the Teacher from New York. How I wish I had kept a journal during those few months! What did I do? How did I juggle the younger children and the older ones? We all know that one-room schoolhouses worked for many years in many communities, but I sorely regret having so few memories of how that particular Sunday school managed to

---

[3] *Sabra* - a native-born Israeli Jew; from the Hebrew Sabēr meaning prickly pear, a common plant in the coastal areas of the country

[4] *Kibbutz* - a collective agricultural settlement in modern Israel, owned and administered communally by its members and on which children are reared collectively

survive. I remember a great deal of noise, action, fun and the weekly return of "The Story," which had to teach Jewishness at its core: history, a value, a tradition or a celebration of ritual. It had to be dramatic, have human interest and enough suspense to keep the room in total silence. It was the promise of this weekly story that earned the cooperation of the older children, who helped organize the games, songs and dances to entertain the younger ones.

In today's terms and professional vocabulary, I was learning about curriculum, classroom management, cooperative learning, non-formal lessons and more. I was learning to think on my feet, to build transition from one activity to the next, to be sensitive to restlessness in my pupils and to build on the leadership of individual pupils. More than anything, I learned that I loved the energy in the room and my ability to keep the energy flowing happily while moving 30 or 40 children from laughing involvement in a board game to the stillness of story time. I was hooked. As so often happens in life, the unexpected lessons of Guelph had nothing to do with living on a *kibbutz* in Israel, and everything to do with discovering my teacher-self.

We left Guelph, realizing that our future would not be linked to *kibbutz*. Yitzchak and I married in late summer and went back to our university studies. He studied engineering in the evenings and did field work during the day. I majored in comparative literature and decided to minor in education. It pains me now to recall the total waste of time those education courses were for my classmates and me. I ask myself why they seemed so irrelevant, especially as I was now teaching Sunday school and loving it. In retrospect, there were two basic weaknesses: course content and teaching style. Education courses at the university did not answer my needs as a young teacher and primarily consisted of frontal lectures on the history, philosophy and theory of education.

Our first child, a boy, was born at the end of that year and I took fewer courses and graduated after five years. Upon my graduation, Yitzchak stopped working and became a full-time engineering student. I took a job as a part-time teacher in a local Jewish school, as the convenient hours and minimal travel time were attractive to me as a young mother. Our son was two and his mother 20 years his senior. Teaching ten hours a week was perfect for me. My pupils were nine and ten-year-olds who came to my classes after a full day at public school. They were tired yet full of energy, sent by parents who wanted to provide a framework of heritage without a personal commitment to practicing ritual. As a result, the children got mixed messages. I was quite young and took the stated mission of the school seriously. In time, more than one parent complained that their children were asking about rituals and ceremonies that Teacher had taught them. The children demanded to know why their parents, who had insisted on sending them to Teacher, were skipping all the good parts!

Was it my own tremendous involvement in motherhood at that time or simply maturity, I wonder, which helped me to learn the next lesson? I realized that conviction is not always enough of a reason to produce conflict and tensions, and that I needed to clarify basic values for myself. I wanted my pupils to know about Jewish practice and to be enthused by the continuity of a thousands-of-years-old tradition. I wanted them to feel the beauty of special days through songs and prayers that would bond them to previous generations. But surely I did not want to estrange them from their parents or create a detachment between home and school. I worked hard to find ways that would both honor the tradition as well as their personal home realities.

I recognized that if I wanted to nurture these children and not impair them in any way, I had to learn to give genuine respect to diverse views. I learned to talk to parents about the complexity of their children's situation, and to consider ways that the involved and caring adults could be true to their convictions yet protective of their young charges. These were lessons far removed from the dull lectures on the history or philosophy of education.

In 1958, my husband and I took the giant step of moving to Israel, which we had been planning since we met in the youth movement, and since we left Guelph and returned to our studies. My husband had graduated as a civil engineer and had several years of experience, while I had continued teaching. We now had three beautiful children – two little boys and a six-month-old infant. We were bursting with hope, excitement, apprehension and the optimism of healthy young people in their late twenties. We decided to travel by ship since we had so many belongings and would need the time on board to recover from the strain of preparation and leave-taking. The scene at the shipyard remains vividly etched in my memory: family and friends coming to see us off, kissing the children, wishing us luck and promising to write accompanied by more hugging.

We arrived in a country my husband had never seen and that I did not remember. We had little money and no jobs. We had a few friends and family members who had settled in Israel, and they became our lifeline, but nonetheless, that first year in Tel Aviv was probably the most difficult year of my life.

I had grown up in a comfortable and fairly close-knit neighborhood. I went to local schools, purchased a house and taught in the same neighborhood. I could not walk down the main street without meeting friends or their parents, pupils or their parents or friends of my parents. In Tel Aviv, I was suddenly invisible and silent on the streets of our new neighborhood. When my husband found a job and began working in water management, the field he had chosen with Israel's needs in mind, and the boys went off to nursery and primary school, our infant daughter and I were left on our own. What a strange and starkly unfamiliar sensation that was. We went out every day and walked for several hours in the sunny and rainless autumn of Tel Aviv. We lived very near the Mediterranean and it was the sea, I believe, that helped me keep my equilibrium that year. We met no one we knew, greeted no one and were not greeted. The voice I heard was my own, talking and singing to the baby, or talking aloud to myself as I pushed the pram along the beachfront. I spoke sternly to myself about how this move had been a dream for a decade or more, and that thousands of years of Jewish history and my own personal family history and my youth movement experience had all converged and led to this walk along the promenade off the Mediterranean Sea. Nevertheless, I was so homesick! I missed my mother! I missed her joy and devotion to our children. I missed my loving brothers, cousins, aunts and many life-long close friends. I missed shopkeepers who greeted me by name and shops that sold foods I knew how to cook. I missed the daily interaction with my best friend who lived upstairs in the two-family house we had bought in partnership. I even missed the occasional summer or autumn rain that would clear the air and make the heat more bearable. We walked along together and alone, as tears streamed down my cheeks. Eventually, the magic of the baby's charm and the beauty of the sea calmed and comforted me, dried the tears, and helped me realize that transitions are never easy and that life was very rich indeed.

An old friend from the Guelph days came to visit from Jerusalem and was disappointed in my less than totally adjusted state of mind. "You need to get back to work," he told me, "you probably miss your teaching as well as everything else." I began to consider the possibility of teaching again. There was a high school only a few minute's walk from where we lived, and I walked in one day and asked if there was a position for an English teacher. Although my training was in English literature and not in teaching English as a second language, I felt confident in my knowledge of the language and in the happy classroom experience I had had for several years. In 1959, there were not many native speakers of English with teaching qualifications, and yet English was a required subject in Israeli schools beginning with the 5th grade. In fact, that school did need an English teacher and I was invited to an interview with the principal.

The shadow of the principal in that neighborhood school in Tel Aviv still hangs over me, remaining a life-long reminder of the centrality of the principal's role. She admitted that there was an opening for an English teacher, but she was reluctant to hire an American as the accent was not one she admired. She would much prefer, she told me, a teacher with British pronunciation, the real English. I was struck dumb, not knowing what to say and not wanting to offend her ears with possible overtones of Americana in my simple Hebrew. She went on to tell me that Israeli teenagers were a very different population from any I had ever taught before and would prove difficult for me to deal with. She had heard that Americans were overly permissive and their classrooms often chaotic. She sighed deeply and reluctantly hired me for the new school year, still two months off. I told her I could teach only ten hours a week as my daughter was not yet two, and that the attraction of the school was its proximity to our home, minimizing the time I would need to be away from the baby. When I arrived for the staff meeting the day before term was to begin, I found that I was scheduled to teach 15 hours per week, split between the school's two campuses, adding another hour per day of travel time.

Two telling scenes from my first year of teaching will complete the portrait of this principal. As I came to know my pupils, it was obvious that their knowledge of English was practically non-existent. The syllabus called for teaching what I considered utter nonsense, for example, memorizing long lists of the masculine and feminine forms of words. Pupils were asked to recite witch-wizard, cow-bull, hen-rooster, and so on. I decided to try teaching the parts of the body, such as arms, head, shoulder, waist, etc. by playing "Simon Says" with them. The room was long and narrow with close to 40 girls arranged in rows. The game involved my saying, "Simon says: hands on head." Obviously, I had to be visible to all the girls. I stood up on the table in front, the class stood, and we played. There was laughter and fun and, I think, a bit of basic learning of terms. This happy scene was interrupted by sudden silence as the door opened and the principal walked in. We all froze. "I was wondering what that terrible noise was," she said before she turned and left. But the look she gave me screamed: "Chaos! Americans!"

The second memory is of a stormy winter morning when the babysitter came a few minutes late. I ran breathless to school, arriving some five minutes late, sopping and bedraggled. Not wanting to take the time to hang my raincoat in the staff room, I hurried to my classroom. The room was stone-still, the principal standing just inside the door, silently. As I entered, the girls' faces turned towards me lit up with apprehension. My school leader-colleague took in my clearly harassed condition and greeted me: "How do you think we can educate pupils to punctuality when their teacher has not yet learned it!?" A snort, a look of deep contempt, and out she went.

I stood there, trying to catch my breath and feel less chilled in body and spirit. I must have been a piteous sight for within a minute the girls swarmed around me. "Don't mind her!" they whispered fiercely. "She's just really mean!" They helped me out of the sopping wet coat and took it to the staff room. They stood as close to me as possible, literally warming and heartwarming me thoroughly with their compassion and affection. These were the Israeli teenagers I had been warned that I would be unable to "deal with."

How much I learned in the six years I taught in that school! The school was for girls who had failed the standard assessment test given towards the end of their primary school life. Consequently, they were offered only a meager choice of subjects in which to major: clerking, practical nursing, and a pre-teaching track leading to a teacher's seminary. This was my introduction to the government policy of directing girls with a poor academic record into the teaching profession. Coming from a city with a strong regard for the graduate degrees in early childhood, I was aghast at the implications of such an upside-down policy. The school did not allow the girls to take full matriculation exams, fearing that their inevitable failure would not reflect gloriously on the school.

Not one girl in that school had ever taken the matriculation exams in English, but I was determined to give them the opportunity. Certainly, they were of average intelligence, serious about the work I gave them, and impressively motivated. The principal fought my plea to have them take the exam, reiterating the shame their assured failure would bring to the school. The class petitioned strongly, several friends on staff supported our wishes and I went so far as to turn to the National Inspector of English. Six was a passing grade for matriculation, with all exams marked by outside examiners. All my 21 girls passed, with the class stars helping to bring the average up to eight! Our triumph was joyous.

The sweetness of that victory over pettiness was to be tasted several times over as I met those girls later in their adult lives. Twenty years later, standing outside my office in the School of Education at Hebrew University, a young woman rushed up to me with shy excitement. "Ora! Ora Zohar! Remember me? I was in your class in...." She was now working toward a graduate degree in the department. I met another of those girls, now a tenured primary school principal, when she enrolled in our Principals' Center. Later, when I spoke to the group passionately about the moral role of educational leaders and their responsibility to build nurturing school cultures, she directed a significant smile my way, full of shared memories and truths. Another woman, taking a graduate level course on Reflective Practice, raised her hand in the midst of the class discussion to announce that everything I was suggesting could indeed be done in schools. She continued ardently, "... and I know that teachers can change their pupils' lives, because my entire life changed when I passed the matriculation exam in English. Then I was able to continue my education and I became a guidance counselor so I could encourage other pupils, just as I was encouraged so many years ago by one special teacher.... whose name is Ora Zohar!" She spoke while looking directly at me with joy, and yes, with love.

Israeli schools have a position, unfamiliar to me from American schools, of pastoral care teacher. This teacher is known as the *Mechanech* (when the teacher is a man), *or Mechanechet,* (when the teacher is a woman). In this Israeli model, one adult staff member is responsible for the comprehensive day-to-day school experience and general well-being of a single class. If a teacher has difficulties with the class or with a pupil, he turns to the pastoral care teacher. If a parent has questions about a child's social or academic progress, the pastoral care teacher is the address at school. All matters of concern are brought to the pastoral care teacher to solve or to address, on either the class or the individual pupil level.

I fell in love with this model and asked to become a *Mechanechet* with a class of my own, in addition to teaching English. The principal was adamant in her refusal: "An American cannot possibly be a *Mechanechet*," she said. "You have to really understand the Israeli mentality to be effective." I had been teaching in that school for five or six years already. My classes had done well academically and socially and I loved the girls. I envied my colleagues who had stronger and deeper ties, or at least the opportunities to develop these. For me this refusal was the last straw and I decided to leave the school. Our family had already moved to another neighborhood and the principal of the prestigious secondary school in the new neighborhood had asked me to teach at his school. I announced my decision to leave to the principal of the school where I taught. "Never!" she retorted. "This is a city school and you can only teach in another city school if I release you. I promise you I won't do that!"

My husband and I talked this over at length and when the City Board of Education confirmed that I could only be assigned to the new school upon release from my present school, we reached a decision. I went to the Board and informed them I would leave the system, preferring not to teach, rather than remain with that principal. Brinksmanship perhaps, but they realized that I was absolutely sincere. Within a few weeks, I was transferred to the new school and came to an understanding with the principal: I would teach English the first year and thereafter, become a *Mechanechet*.

One question I have often asked teachers is, "What baggage have you brought with you from your previous roles in life and how do you integrate this into your present role?" The "baggage" I brought to the new school was extremely helpful. I brought years of successful classroom teaching, a sense of closeness to the pupils in my classes, an educated appreciation of the new principal's leadership, and eagerness to develop the *Mechanech* role to the fullest. The years in Israel had helped me to feel a part of the country, and I believe, my nuclear family was crucial to my personal development. During the years of conflict and frustration at the first school, both my husband and children were a comfort to me, encouraging me in my fight to take students to matriculation, and finally, deciding together that the environment was too distressing. My own joyous mothering of three bright and delightful youngsters enriched my life on a daily basis and honed many skills that were to prove critical in my new role. In addition, the experiences my own children had had with their pastoral care teachers had sensitized me to the enormous potential of the role, for good and for bad. I had seen good ones enhance the school lives of my children and had also experienced the misery caused by someone unsuited to the role.

As agreed, I became a *Mechanechet* in the second year at the new school. My class was an 11th grade group of 29 girls majoring in languages which required them to take full matriculation in all regular subjects and advanced matriculation in English and French. They were intelligent, thoughtful and spirited teenagers and we fell in love with each other immediately. I taught English five hours a week, had one slotted hour per week for a multipurpose class session, and met one-on-one with girls on both a structured and as needed basis. Practically speaking, I regularly invited individual girls to chat about school life or life in general. In addition, any girl or group of girls who felt the need to talk about an issue or problem with me could simply initiate a meeting. The issues we touched on were myriad, ranging from anger toward a teacher or classmate to despair over an emotional entanglement, to questions of faith or difficult family situations.

Buildings on the school campus were overflowing and the school was short a classroom. As my class was the smallest in the 11th grade, our homeroom was assigned to a wooden hut on campus, removed from the main buildings. The girls were outraged. They resented the inferior facilities, the distance from the bathrooms, and the heat in the summer and dankness during the rainy season. Clearly, this had to be turned to our advantage, and I set about presenting this challenge to the girls. We decided to turn that hut into the most desirable piece of real estate on campus. We painted it and put up curtains. I added a colorful cloth and a wrought iron plant holder to my desk. One after another, decorative plants filled our space. We painted the front door a startling orange and put up a wooden plaque with our class name. In the best Tom Sawyer tradition, all this activity attracted much attention – and then envy – from classes housed in the usual classrooms in the large cement building. Pupils came by to ooh and aah, and the girls were jubilant. The following year, when we were invited to be housed in a classroom in the main building, there was a unanimous decision to reject the offer and stay in our own darling hut.

Relationships developed as well with the girls' parents, and I was often reminded of my long-ago experiences in New York and situations which called for the basic life-skills of empathy and tact. With parents too, issues ranged from clear-cut academic achievement to concerns regarding social development or future career decisions. In time, some parent meetings became open discussions about care for elderly parents or a sibling's learning disabilities. As in most schools in Israel, *Mechanchim*[5] remained with their class for two years, so that I had my class, and the classes that followed, for their junior and senior years of high school.

In June of that year, the Six-Day War broke out and together we faced those tense weeks before and during the war. In the days after the Suez Canal was closed to international traffic and Nasser expelled the U.N. troops from Sinai, every Israeli in the country watched the desperate diplomatic efforts to avoid war – watched in growing fear and anxiety as one effort after another proved fruitless and the international community proved impotent, once again. In late May, schools had to balance normalcy and logic. We studied and taped up windows in our school, the neighboring primary school and the nearby hospital. The boys were assigned to dig trenches around the schoolyard and to stack sandbags. We had air raid drills and sang classic Israeli songs, including the new Naomi Shemer hit, *Jerusalem the Golden*. Her prophetic song that electrified the country was written after a 19-year interval without access to the Old City's holy sites and only several weeks before Jerusalem became a united city once again.

The war had many national and personal consequences for all of us. A beloved brother of one of our girls was killed in action, a colleague lost a son and many graduates were among the dead and wounded. Our family's intensely personal response was a need to replenish and to bring new life where there had been so much death. Our fourth child was born at the end of 1968, bringing the unrivaled joy of a baby into the house and the dimension of renewal to our people.

That first class had graduated and my girls were scattered throughout the country completing their National Service. When David was born,

---

[5] Plural form

my husband sent a telegram to the town where a group of girls was serving. Two days later the girls began streaming into my hospital room along with my new class of girls. We were three women to a room at a private maternity hospital in Tel Aviv. My roommates marveled at the stream of youngsters coming to visit me and at my own delight in seeing them.

I share these stories to clarify what I so strongly believe: relationships between schoolchildren and the adults who choose to spend their lives in schools can be a lifelong source of nurturing and growth for all concerned. Both my high school pupils as well as my graduate students have enriched my life, and continue to do so until today.

Before long, it became evident at the new school that my classroom teaching approach and techniques differed from those of my colleagues. Early suspicions turned to respect as matriculation results returned and the 100 or so girls I taught each year did very well. This led the principal to offer me the chair of the department. This was a mistake on his part, worsened only on my part by accepting the position. I had no training in supervision and had not yet become a reflective practitioner. The position was multi-dimensional, involving department meetings on curriculum or policy, visiting classrooms for general supervision and feedback. The first was fairly simple, as I had attended such meetings for several years. However, my visits to colleagues' classes were a total waste of time for me and certainly worthless for their professional development. It became clear to me that I could evaluate the lesson unfolding before me. One lesson was alive and flowing while another was torture for everyone in the room, pupils, teacher and observer. But why? What facilitated and what inhibited learning? What created that warm sense of cooperation in a group, and what led to the atmosphere of an armed camp in another group? I did not know. And my only feedback to colleagues was a weak, "Thank you for having me," which was harmless but not at all helpful.

During this busy and productive period of personal and professional life, I was asked to train new English teachers at a university. I took the position on condition that I would be wholly responsible for both the theoretical methodology of teaching a second language as well as for the required fieldwork of classroom observation and student teaching. This forced me to consider how to make classroom observation a structured learning experience for observers, for example noting a teacher's use of the blackboard or use of non-verbal responses to pupils. Slowly, I began to perceive the threads of teaching that created a pleasing tapestry or an unraveling mess. Together, my students and I learned and attempted to put what we learned into practice. Through simulation, role-play and videotaped micro-lessons we practiced the Art of Teaching. Does practice really make perfect? Perhaps not, but minimally we demonstrated enormous respect for the complexity of the profession in which we were involved.

I also worked with classroom teachers who had graciously agreed to have our students observe and later teach their classes. We discussed what would be helpful to novices entering the profession, how to create diverse lessons for them to observe and what post-lesson discussions would include. This was a new kind of collegial dialogue that made me aware of the essential isolation of so much of our work as classroom teachers and of our thirst to share, discuss and consider professional issues together.

As my students graduated and began teaching, we learned through their experiences that the culture of a school is far more powerful than the personal culture of new teachers entering a school, regardless of how dedicated and determined they are. Oh, how the tears gushed over the phone! Lessons we had planned were not succeeding and neighboring teachers did not appreciate noisy classrooms. Confidence was being eroded and help was needed.

It became increasingly clear that in-service education was essential to helping my graduates. It would be directly helpful to them and, if older colleagues were to attend courses as well, the established practice might be influenced. I thus took on what eventually became known as a popular summer in-service program tailored to English teachers throughout Israel. The two-week program, which met daily from nine to four, included dormitory accommodation for out-of-town participants. Nearly 60 teachers participated that first summer, while each summer thereafter the program drew close to 200 participants. It was a rich and varied program with lectures on literature and linguistics offered by my university colleagues, workshops on topics such as developing writing skills for secondary school pupils and my own sessions with the entire group on personal reflection.

By this time, after a decade of work in Israeli schools as a classroom teacher, *Mechanechet*, department chair and teacher trainer, I had learned that many classroom and school concerns are not directly connected to teaching a specific subject, but rather to the interactions between the staff who share school life. I began to search for ways in which practicing teachers could enrich these interactions, making the hours spent in schools more significant, more valuable and more important than the teaching of cow-bull, present-past continuous tense or even beautiful poetry.

The summer courses offered me the opportunity to experiment, implement and evaluate. My work with both would-be and practicing teachers was exciting and rewarding, and above all, totally autonomous. I had complete freedom of thought.

I could assess the success or failure of experimental units and had total responsibility for their redesign and re-teaching. Feedback from students and participating teachers helped me to understand, change and refocus. As I put the finishing touches on the two-week program for the summer of 1973, I had no idea that my professional life would soon take a dramatic turn.

A few days before the summer program was to open, I received a call from the Ministry of Education. Could I please, they asked, fit an overseas Ministry guest into our program? The guest, they went on, was a well-known Dean of Education in the United States, keen to see any operating educational program in Israel. It was early July and all schools were closed. The only program available in English was the one I was coordinating. "Out of the question," I replied, "all our hours are programmed and our lecturers have been registered for months." Out of pure curiosity, however, I asked the name of the Ministry's guest. It was Dwight Allen, then Dean of the School of Education of the University of Massachusetts at Amherst. I knew his work and had been captivated by his book on Microteaching. In fact, I had been offering a seminar on microteaching for several years as part of the teacher training courses. Clearly, it would be impossible to let this opportunity pass. I decreased my own teaching hours and Dwight became the star of that summer course, to be fondly remembered for many years by those teachers fortunate enough to have studied with him.

At lunch on his second day with us, Dwight dropped his bombshell. He had watched me in action for two days. He had asked me many questions about where I was going professionally and we had spoken about my basic convictions and interests. He wondered why I did not have a doctorate. I explained to him that in Israel, it was impossible to do graduate work across disciplines. My own undergraduate and graduate studies had been in literature. To become a doctoral student in education, I would have to backtrack and take many courses in education. I was unwilling to do this and had resigned myself to the situation. "No," Dwight said, "you need a degree, it's like a union card for you. You are doing marvelous work in teacher education and you can only advance professionally if you have a graduate degree in teacher education. Come to the University of Massachusetts at Amherst, and take your doctoral degree there." I thanked him and smiled, knowing how impossible this was – we had four children, no money, and jobs in Israel. Yet he was persuasive. He offered me a complete doctoral fellowship and a small stipend. I would work in the Clinic to Improve University Teaching on campus while studying. He made me promise to talk it over with my husband and return to him within a week. That was in July, 1973.

Yitzchak and I talked all night long for several nights. It was clear to both of us that this was the chance of a lifetime for my professional development. Yitzhak was as determined as Dwight had been. "We'll find ways to do it as a family," he said. And we did – late August found me en route to the U.S.A, 15 years after leaving for Israel. I went with the two younger children, aged 5 and 15; the older boys had opted not to come as they were already studying at university. We rented out our Jerusalem apartment to cover the rent in Amherst, and the boys joined my mother for the weekends, to her great joy. The Jewish holidays were several weeks off and we decided that Yitzchak would stay with the boys and my mother through the holidays and then join us in Amherst. It is perhaps worth noting here that the Ministry of Health, where Yitzchak was well established as Assistant Chief Water Quality Engineer, was strongly opposed to his taking a year's leave to go to Amherst. They had difficulty accepting the fact that in this case the man was following his wife, rather than the very familiar reverse. They suggested he stay in Israel and they would provide a housekeeper!

Early September found the three of us living in a townhouse in Echo Hill in Amherst, Massachusetts, approximately 15 minutes away from the University of Massachusetts campus. David was enrolled in kindergarten and Naava in the local high school. I was a doctoral student, a single parent and a total stranger once again.

It is impossible to recount this period without writing about the absolute trauma of that October. Some four weeks into our move, on October 6th, 1973, the Yom Kippur War broke out in Israel. The children and I knew that our three men were involved. The phone lines to Israel were overloaded and no airline would give us seats bound for a war zone. We were helpless and desperate. Our extended family in America called constantly to give us support and love, but they could not offer what we craved – information about Yitzchak, Zvi and Noam.

We knew that both boys were in the Sinai, and American headlines and TV coverage were filled with the tragic views of the first week of that terrible war. Several days into the war, we finally reached my mother in Jerusalem, and learned that that very day both boys had been heard from and that Yitzchak was away in his capacity as Emergency Water Manager. He was released weeks later, and in late November arrived in Amherst to join us. David had become somewhat acculturated in those two months, and as Yitzchak pulled up in front of our house he began shouting wildly - in English - to all his friends, "It's my Daddy! It's my Daddy!"

Against this backdrop of war, anxiety and mourning for the boys that our tiny country had lost, I traveled my own new road as student after so many years as teacher.

The contrast between the reality of 1973 Israel and 1973 Amherst is almost too stark to describe. In the first weeks of the war, I walked to class weeping while crossing the beautiful campus. I saw the glory of the New England autumn and the frolicking students around me as I walked on, haunted by imagined scenes and activities of all the teenagers I knew and loved in Israel. Where all news and reports from home were sad and gloomy, the Amherst reality was a blinding dazzling light. What lightness of mood! Such freedom of thought and action, informality of student-faculty relations, an overwhelming sense of interest and motivation, liveliness of class discussions and intoxication with the library and new-found reading material. All this was joy, possibly more keenly felt under the circumstances.

Beyond the shared experiences with fellow students, my own connection to the Clinic to Improve University Teaching was the core of my training that year as well as my later work. When Dwight had invited me to Amherst and told me about work in the Clinic, I had no idea what was involved. He had told me it was a clinic to help university faculty improve their teaching, and I would be one of ten T.I.S. (Teaching Improvement Specialists). I smiled and said, "Well, I guess I could work with anyone involved in foreign language teaching." He laughed. I added, "Well, perhaps I could also work with people teaching poetry and drama." He laughed again, and as I began my training and then my work in the clinic, I understood his amusement. Individual faculty members came to the clinic through many routes: some were encouraged to come by their departmental chair, others had heard of the process from colleagues, still others came on their own, having heard or read of the clinic's work. Each client was assigned to a T.I.S, who became a personal aide in the client's efforts to improve his teaching. My clients that year included professors of economics, Chinese history, geography and education. I found the process fascinating. Together, we moved through the clinic structure of initial interview, extensive questionnaire, classroom observations (when desired) and consideration of alternate teaching strategies. I learned, thoroughly and forever, what I had been sensing in my work in Israel: the art and complexity of teaching is interdisciplinary and subject matter is but one element of many. It was intensely challenging for me to work with Tom, my first client, and to see how much progress we could make together. Each client was a new challenge and a pleasure.

As the year went on, I saw the fruits of the Clinic approach to teacher training. I wondered how it could be adapted to my own country's needs for the improvement of primary and secondary school teaching. While I enjoyed the one-to-one relationship with a client, clearly this model was not economically feasible for the Israeli education system. Could the process be adapted to a group setting? Could a T.I.S. work with a group, facilitating both individual and group growth? If subject matter was not of the essence, could teachers of different subjects find that teaching strategies useful in an economics class, for example, could be equally useful in a class on Chinese history?

I decided to find out. I wrote to a principal of a private Jewish high school in New York City, offering to give a four-day workshop to a group of his teachers. My Israeli identity was a plus as was my doctoral status at the University of Massachusetts. He invited me for a discussion, after which he decided that he would free his ten department chairpersons for four days and give them to me for Staff Development. Yitzchak and the children wished me luck and I was off to New York for the first pilot project of my dissertation. The four days were wildly successful, the written feedback was glowing and my own sense of having found a way to be helpful was confirmed.

At this point I first envisioned a national center which would provide a structured professional growth program for teachers of kindergarten through 12th grades, regardless of subject specialty. This center would build nurturing support groups for teachers in which issues, concerns and problems would be raised and faced together. Groups would be led by trained center staff whose roles would be clearly facilitative. The perception of teaching would incorporate both the Amherst Clinic's approach (Allen, 1969) and Carl Rogers' concept of facilitation (Rogers, 1961). It seemed to me that this synthesis would prove both attractive and helpful with groups of teachers. I envisioned the new center based at a university, supported and recognized by the Ministry. I wrote a long proposal to my university. I wrote in detail about my vision, explaining how it would not be prohibitive as I would train the staff and direct the clinic within the bounds of the position I already held.

The proposal was rejected. I was reminded that I did wonderful work with teachers of English and was sorely missed. My strong statements of working with non-language teachers on issues less related to foreign language acquisition were laughed away. The basic response was: "Come home, Ora, all is forgiven and your job awaits you."

Years later, when I was happily established as the Director of the flourishing National Center for Staff Development at Hebrew University in Jerusalem, the president at the university where I had previously taught reiterated that he could not forgive me for leaving, nor the School of Education for allowing me to leave. In retrospect, it was the best thing that could have happened, since several years earlier we had already moved to Jerusalem.

Chapter 2
The Story of the National Center
for Staff Development

I have been grateful to Mr. Goldberg for decades but it is only recently that I have realized my deeper debt. Here is the story. Henry Goldberg was the principal of the afternoon Hebrew school affiliated with the large prestigious Temple in my neighborhood in Brooklyn. Many families wished to have their sons' Bar Mitzva ceremonies take place in that Temple and agreed to the prerequisite policy demanding several years of study in the Hebrew school. Thus, the school was brimming over with hundreds of youngsters between the ages of nine to thirteen.

I was an undergraduate with very limited teaching experience but known as an active leader in the local Zionist youth movement. I was delighted to be invited to teach several afternoons a week. An incident at a staff meeting early in the year first generated my gratitude to Mr. Goldberg. There was an interesting discussion in Hebrew that I tried to join, but soon I switched to English to make sure I would be understood. An Israeli teacher turned to Mr. Goldberg in annoyance and said in perfect rapid Hebrew, "I don't understand how Ora can be a teacher in this school. Why, she barely knows Hebrew herself!" I was mortified by the enormity of the truth of her charge and sat silent, wondering how it could be refuted. Mr.Goldberg looked at her with a strange look and said gently, "Well, you see, in this school we teach children, and Ora knows children very well!" I was saved and thanked him in my heart forever.

Introduction

The National Center for Staff Development at the School of Education at the Hebrew University opened its doors in 1977 and remained active until about 2005. In this chapter I tell the story of the Center's early stages, its expansion and its overall scope of activity - including staff development workshops in Israel and abroad. Later chapters will discuss other facets of the Center's work including the Principals' Center, and RICH – a value-based English language curriculum.

Finding an Institutional Base for the Center

I returned to Israel in 1974 with a clear vision of the Center but without an institutional base. For two years, I facilitated a number of intensive seminars at Bar Ilan University, Hebrew University and the Ministry of Education. In these seminars, I conveyed the working assumptions I had learned in Amherst, unfamiliar in Israel at the time:

1. Teaching is not a mystique, but rather a collection of specific skills that can be identified, evaluated, practiced and thus improved.

2. Despite documented teacher resistance to supervision, the inherent human need for self-actualization could be harnessed to teacher improvement.

3. In total contrast to the Israeli model, the process was not subject-centered but teacher-centered. This meant that teachers of different disciplines could attend the same course, or that the entire staff of a school could work together to improve the overall quality of teaching at a school.

While training was received enthusiastically, finding an institutional partner who would risk investing in our unconventional mode of work was a challenge. In 1976 Professor Seymour Fox, then Dean of the School of Education at Hebrew University, defied local academic and educational wisdom and offered me a full time position on the faculty "to do what you want to do to improve teaching and schools." It was an enormous step forward for me. The idea of a National Center to focus on the improvement of education located in the Hebrew University School of Education was born. Being associated with this prestigious institution and being physically situated on campus contributed to the attractiveness of our work in the eyes of many potential clients, thereby contributing significantly to our success in the years to come.

Building the Team

The vision of the National Center was quite clear to me now; how to turn it into reality was less so. I realized that the first step had to be the creation of a talented and dedicated staff who would become the leaders of future workshops at the Center. In October 1977, a group of ten women began a 200-hour training course with me at the university. Six were teachers of English whom I knew well, while four came highly recommended by a colleague. Five of that original group served on the staff for the next 20 years. All of these women were bright and successful classroom teachers with years of experience and considerable self-confidence.

Ruth taught high school level English and was responsible for training future teachers at a local teacher's seminary. Born in South Africa, Rachel had enormous knowledge, an exhausting work ethic, a unique rapport with her students of varied backgrounds in a developing area of the country, and a capacity to read and internalize new knowledge that left us all breathless. Bina taught Bible in a technical high school. She brought a sharp mind, a keen eye for reality and a strong personality to the group. Malka taught geography and history in a comprehensive high school for girls. She was practical, direct, and devoted to her students.

Chava G. was an old friend who had come to live in Israel with her husband and three young sons. She had taught in the U.S. but had since trained as a librarian and had to be wooed away from her current job. Her intelligence, insights and integrity were too valuable to lose. I knew she would be the great asset to the Center that she indeed became for many years to come.

Chava Z. was an unknown, arriving on the first day of the program without the extensive interview that all other participants had undergone. We had spoken on the phone and agreed that time pressures dictated that we simply take a chance on each other and meet on the first day. She was a guidance counselor in a primary school and a woman of culture, creativity and humor. She would travel the world with me in overseas assignments and accompany me through every step of the Center's development in the years to follow.

We met every Monday from nine to three for the entire year. My own goals for the year were well defined, but designing a program that would realize those goals was an exciting challenge. I wanted to create a learning experience that would distill the experiences of my previous decade of professional growth. I wanted the ten women in that first group to change their sense of personal and professional identity, to follow a course comparable to my own which had obviously been effected through a natural process of life, chance and luck. I wanted each of them to shift away from thinking of herself as a teacher of English, Bible, or geography, and to regard herself as a Master of Teaching. It was radical at the time to suggest that their teaching expertise in one subject area might qualify them to help teachers of other subjects. Even today, so many years later, interdisciplinary studies are not the norm, and both university studies and in-service courses are subject-based.

If they approved that radical concept, I also wanted the program to give them the skills and confidence to facilitate professional growth in workshops the Center would offer. These would be similar to the Amherst Clinic model, augmented by modifications made for the pilot groups I had led in New York City and in Israel.

It was an exciting year for all of us and a year of tremendous growth for each of us individually. Mid-year, we gave several workshops to test our skills and the curriculum we had developed. The results were successful enough to encourage us to search for clients for the following year.

At this time, we made a decision that was to prove crucial for many years: to work in pairs and co-lead workshops. This decision was the result of several strands of thought. Frankly, staff members were terrified of facing a group of teachers of various subject matter and suggesting that they could be helpful. My own experiences in that area had been within the supportive structure of the Clinic, and had been in a one-to-one framework. I understood the panic. In addition, I personally saw a great advantage to modeling Team Teaching and to the deliberate pairing of women with very different teaching styles. I wanted to avoid any sense of our Center presenting a particular style as The Teaching Style. Co-leading also gave us greater flexibility in terms of splitting a group for half a session, or for all kinds of alternative teaching. The intense team-teaching – planning, deciding who will do what, feedback after sessions, reflecting on how sessions went and on how what had happened would now affect the next session – proved stimulating and rewarding beyond description.

Branching Out: Workshops in the Field

Our first workshops were designed for an entire school staff, or – in very small cities – for the combined staffs of two schools. The following year, while the original leaders conducted ten workshops for teachers in different parts of Israel, a second group of ten teachers was trained.

Over the next few years, we reached ever-expanding school populations, ranging from preschools to universities, and including role-focused training programs for *Mechanchim*, department chairmen and regional supervisors. All of these programs were contracted for with the Ministry of Education or with local municipalities.

We also offered several shorter workshops within the University for beginning lecturers, and for Nursing School and Dental School faculty. During years of heightened immigration from the Soviet Union, we developed a special program for new immigrant teachers, helping them adapt to the culture of Israeli schools and students.

As word of our ability to work across subject lines spread, we received invitations for workshops from schools across the country that represented all sectors of Israeli society: Moslem, Christian, Jewish secular, Jewish religious, urban and *kibbutz*. We trained third and fourth groups of workshop leaders in order to meet the requests that flowed in from the field.

The following map graphically represents the reach of the Center's work within Israel.

Working with Jewish Schools Abroad

One day in 1982, Professor Fox approached me, saying: "Ora, we're hosting a group of lay leaders from Australia and I want you to spend an hour or two with them. I want them to realize that at the Melton Center for Jewish Education at the Hebrew University we're not just about Jewish Education, but about education in general." "Fine," I said, "but they're not teachers or connected to schools, so what shall we do in that time?" "It doesn't matter," Professor Fox told me, "anything that will get them passionate about education and schools." After much thought we decided to introduce one of our favorite poems, Miss Darcy, about a terrible first grade teacher and her impact on the five-year-old speaker (see Chapter 5). It was a turbulent session to an amazed group of lay leaders.

Professor Fox met me in the hall two hours later. "OK, Ora," he greeted me, "start packing, you're going to Australia." And I did, nine times. Our intervention there is described in detail in chapter 8.

Our staff's ability to work with an inclusive school staff was valuable for Jewish schools outside of Israel. Our successes led to years of invitations from England, Australia (Sidney, Melbourne, Perth), South Africa (Johannesburg, Cape Town), the United States (New York, Baltimore), Canada (Toronto), Mexico, and Hungary. In addition, many of these and other trainees from around the world were hosted at the Hebrew University in Jerusalem where they were able to benefit from many other educational resources.

The following map portrays the international scope of the Center's work.

Chapter 3
Discovering Significance Through Reflection

When I trained English teachers, I was fortunate to know many veteran teachers who agreed to host my students as guest observers for a number of weeks. Each of these teachers was excellent. They worked in a variety of schools, offering a wide range of exposure for novice teachers. I was grateful for their cooperation and advised my students to observe carefully, ask clear questions and listen closely to the wisdom of their practiced elders.

Week after week when the students returned, we discussed their experiences and I was terribly disappointed! My students reported that when they asked teachers why they had behaved in a particular manner, given a specific assignment or chosen to respond in a certain way, the frequent reply was, "Oh, you learn with time what works and then you go with that. It's all about experience and you'll gain that too." This struck me as unhelpful advice to new teachers and it revealed a non-reflective – and to my mind, unprofessional – attitude toward their work.

Reflection is central to all of the Center's work with professional educators regardless of their particular role. More than 100 years ago, John Dewey (1916) wrote of the importance of professional deliberation for teachers, the need to reflect on their actions and to consider the consequences. For Dewey this was a moral imperative for educators.

In the century since then, the field of teacher preparation and in-service education has seen many changes, revolving fashions and a rich variety of models. Since 1980, the wheel has turned again, and Donald Schon's work and writings about reflective practice (1983, 1987) have greatly influenced teacher education programs at teaching colleges and universities around the world. Emphasis is now centered on teacher thoughtfulness, recollection of personal actions, clarification of beliefs and values and acceptance of responsibility for consequences in a particular setting. A teacher's basic questions have shifted away from the substance and content of teaching, concentrating rather on the values that drive the teaching process and discovery of a personalized teaching approach.

Professional reflection is part of each teacher's personal search for meaning and each teacher will express her concerns in a unique and personal voice. As a reflective practitioner, there are many levels of questions to be asked before each teaching session. In my overall capacity as a teacher, I need to examine: What is important to me? How can I get kids to respect each other? How do I want to interact with students, colleagues and parents in particular situations? What do I hope to accomplish this year?

Initial class sessions demand specific questions: Who are my new students, both personally and professionally? What prior school experiences do they bring with them? If this is a graduate class, they may not know each other; if it is a school-based workshop, teachers may know each other only within the confines of the staff room. The reality of each type of class demands very different reflection and preparation, yet the basics must be interwoven. Although the traditional focus on subject matter has sometimes blurred these questions, the Center's work attempted to change this balance.

In our workshops, a common means of encouraging reflection was the use of memories, recall and sharing. We always struggled to find the most appropriate and effective strategy. Should group participants write memories in a journal? Should they share them verbally with a partner, or perhaps in trios for a richer experience? And how much time should we allot for each of these?

I AM A CAMERA

An example of the way in which reflection was used in the Center to highlight the significance of every child was documented by Aviva Pinchuk in the following description of the I AM A CAMERA exercise used in training group facilitators:

> At our bi-weekly staff meetings, Ora often presented new educational research and/or a new introspective activity. That

week, listed on the board, was the item I AM A CAMERA. I could not begin to imagine what surprise activity Ora had planned for us!

Ora asked us to imagine one of our classes exactly the way it looks on a normal teaching day. I chose a tenth grade class comprising almost 40 pupils that I had taught the year before. She told us to position ourselves somewhere in the classroom, take out a camera, aim and shoot. We were all busy clicking our shutters not knowing where this was going. After a few moments, we were asked to look at the photo we just took, noticing all our pupils, where they were sitting, what they were doing at the time the shutter was pressed.

We were all curious and amused and Ora continued. "Surely, many of the images in your picture came out very clear and sharp. Share your information and impressions of one of these sharp images with your neighbor." It felt good to talk about a pupil I felt I really knew well and to hear my colleague's report of her sharp image! The conversations in the room were all lively and animated.

Then came the bummer! Ora continued with the next exercise. "Look at your photograph again. Find the blurry images, where the focus was somewhat off, or where the faces are hidden by the person in front, or where the light didn't quite reach. Choose one of these images and write a few sentences and questions. Ask yourself why this image is not as sharp as the others."

The atmosphere in the room suddenly changed. Everyone became very somber and pensive.

I immediately thought of two immigrant girls who always sat together in the corner of the room, not disturbing the class in any way, but always indifferent and apathetic. They never showed any interest in what was going on in the class but were always very respectful. In a class of just under 40, how could I get to everyone?

In threes, we were asked to share our blurry images and to discuss ways to sharpen the focus. After listening to the suggestions of my partners, I realized there was much I could have done to involve these girls more. Unfortunately, I was no longer teaching that class. There was nothing I could do to help those particular girls. However, from that learning experience I learned the value of personal talks with all my pupils, sometimes even asking permission from their other teachers for a few extra minutes.

I carry the unfocused images of those two girls in my head to this day. They served as a reminder for the continuation of my teaching career. From that day on, I never walked into class without my camera!

CLOSURES

Another example of facilitating reflection is an exercise we call CLOSURES. In the life of a school, and in the lives of teachers and their classes, many and varied closures are experienced – the end of a class, a subject unit, a semester, and of course the end of the school year. In our workshops, we provide our participants, whether they be kindergarten teachers, schoolteachers, university instructors, principals or supervisors, with the opportunity to reflect upon the closing year relating to all the different aspects of their job performance.

We open the session on CLOSURES by asking pairs to share: "A closure that was easy or difficult for me."

Having set the tone with a nostalgic memory, we ask the group to reflect upon the closing school year. We do this by slowly dictating introspective questions about the many different aspects of the individual's professional performance. The actual writing of the questions (rather than distributing a handout) generates the beginning of thinking. The atmosphere in the room changes. Nothing can be heard but the soft voice of the workshop leader accompanied by the movement of pen on paper. This activity takes time and more time is needed as participants absorb the questions and reflect upon their mental responses. We then ask the participants to evaluate their functioning during the course of the year on a scale of 1-3.

When we feel they are ready to work, we invite the participants to sit in small groups and to share one strength and one area each would like to strengthen, asking for suggestions from the group members.

At the conclusion of this working activity, we invite responses from all the members. Year after year, we hear responses like, "I never had such an opportunity to **think** about my work..." or "I got a wonderful suggestion from my group and I plan to try it next year..."

We might conclude by suggesting to the group that such an activity could be tried in the classroom as well. Some teachers will volunteer immediately to rewrite the questions for use in the classroom for an end of the year activity. The questions have to be appropriate for the individual group.

As an example, we have listed below the questions we presented in our Principals' Center. A principal, upon reaching the end of the school year, not only celebrates the end of the year. He or she also has the opportunity and obligation to take stock. The principal is preoccupied with many crucial questions at the end of the year. He asks himself questions relating to different categories of his job performance. He asks himself about the people for whom he is responsible, about the school organization and about himself.

About the groups of workers in the school, he asks:

- What is the nature of my relationship with my teaching staff? With my management team? With parents? With students? With the municipality?
- Did I take initiative in the relationship?
- Was there cooperation?
- Were my responses effective?
- Was I a good model of behavior and leadership?

About individuals in the school, he asks:

- Did I pay attention to the new teacher, to the veteran teacher?
- Did I have a relationship with a certain parent?
- How did I work with the vice principal? With the school counselor? With the secretary? With the janitor?
- Did I sense the distress of a teacher or student?
- Was I always sufficiently accessible to those who needed me?
- Did I encourage and enable people in the school to grow?
- Did I relate also to the personal side?

About the school's organization and its functions, he asks:

- Did we live up to our educational program?

- Did we create our own unique programs?

- Did everyone know the school's goals?

- How did I cope with new challenges during the year?

- Was building maintenance up to par?

- Did I manage the budget well?

And about himself he asks:

- Did I find ways to learn and advance professionally?

- Was I accessible to my family and friends?

- Did I take good advantage of leisure time?

- Did I learn from experience and from the experience of others?

REFLECTIVE WRITING

Iri Kessel was the principal of a large regional secondary school when we met years ago when he was a member of the first cohort of principals in our fledgling Principals' Center. We meet from time to time and usually talk about people and experiences from the Center, family news or educational issues about which we both care. Iri had been reading many chapters of this book during the writing and was giving me feedback. "You know," he said, "I am enjoying the book as it takes me back to the fun we all had together and how much I learned from the other more experienced principals. The book describes many of the different FORMS we worked with (see chapter five) and have since taken into our own work with our staffs. They in turn use many of these FORMS in their own teaching." I smile happily. "But", he says, "It's all very well to write about the popular ones: MENU, MISSING, MEMBER, but I am personally somewhat disappointed that you barely mention a FORM that I find myself appreciating and using more and more as time goes on."

"Really?" I say amazed. "What FORM is that?"

"The FORM of WRITING," Iri tells me. "You gave us specific assignments to write in a personal professional journal and it was terribly difficult for me at first but then I got used to it and it taught me a great deal about myself and my professional development. As principals, most of the writing we are asked to do entails reports describing school programs, projects, and problems or letters to the Ministry or to parents. We knew what each needed to know or what we wanted to know from them. Suddenly, you asked us to write in a totally different way and I remember thinking , 'What can I write about that?' Then my pen would start writing, helping me to recall, organize, clarify and evaluate my thoughts and experiences. Journal writing for me is a powerful tool for real professional reflection."

During the course of any school day, teachers are exposed to a wide range of experiences demanding instant and appropriate responses; a pupil's sudden outburst; a disagreement with a colleague; a flood in the classroom; a meeting with a parent, an announcement of a new regulation by the Ministry, or an impromptu birthday party in class - to name a few! To all these myriad situations, the teacher is expected to react wisely and instantly! The next morning, the process starts all over again with a new series of events to react to. There is no time for on-the-spot reflection and little time if any for reflection between school days.

An effective tool for professional reflection is JOURNAL WRITING. We ask our participants in the workshops to start their daily journals by describing the events of the day, the lessons, interaction with the pupils/colleagues/parents, staff meetings and so on. At our next session together we ask for comments about their JOURNAL WRITING. It's amazing, they often comment, how descriptive writing eases the way into more emotional, insightful writing, opening the doors to professional reflection!

At this point, we might ask if anyone would like to "share a page." This often leads the group into constructive discussions on how the teacher handled a particular situation and/or advice and suggestions for a plan of action.

Often in our workshops, we will ask for very brief writings to reflect and to demonstrate the power of the pen. For example, we might ask participants to complete sentences such as, *Looking ahead I...*or-*Looking back I...*

Another writing exercise is to think of a dilemma involving work. One participant wrote and read to us the following:

The biggest dilemma for me is when one of my children is home sick. I feel torn between two obligations. Sometimes I am angry with the child for being sick and I take out my frustrations on him!

The fact that she took out her anger on her child was a revelation to her! Needless to say, she got a lot of support and encouragement from the group. In the words of Roland Barth (1990):

We don't write to be understood; we write to understand!

Conclusion

Does reflective practice take up a great deal of time, both before and after real classroom time? Yes it does. Is it worth the time? Obviously. At the heart of reflective practice is the ability to move beyond intuition and to gain clarity regarding the emotional and cognitive processes that generate our decisions and actions, of which we may be barely aware. By developing our capacity to reflect – before, during and after our action in any specific setting – we can become far more effective as professionals, and more significant in the lives of our students. Simultaneously, while reflection is the key to our professional practice, it is also a means for personal growth.

Chapter 4
SET INDUCTIONS – Setting the Stage for Learning

Significant learning does not just happen coincidentally; it is a product of meticulous planning. One critical component of planning for significant learning is the use of what we call the SET INDUCTION. We use SET INDUCTIONS to introduce a new unit that may include any number of class sessions. Examples of units in our work include helping others to grow, building a nurturing environment, professional burnout, and school violence. All of these are central units that will occupy us for a number of lessons. Each of these deserves a SET INDUCTION.

We imagine a SET INDUCTION to be like the music being played as we enter the theater. It sets the emotional tone of the play that we are about to see; it prepares us for the mood even as we settle into our seats; it is with us as the curtain goes up.

We may bring a song, an anecdote, an item of jewelry or clothing, a toy, tool, stuffed animal, food, concept, quote... but it is always related to the issue or theme we want to think about and work on in our ongoing search for professional development.

The best way to understand what we mean by SET INDUCTIONS is to illustrate them with concrete examples from our workshops.

Tsunami

Tsunami is written on the board. Note that it is a fairly new word and ask what it means. Several people tell what they think.... it is serious trouble, it causes great havoc and damage...We add EWS to our board and all discuss what we have learned about Early Warning Systems and how they have saved lives where they have been installed. We then ask participants to share their response to the new board sentence: TSUNAMI IN MY CLASS or SCHOOL.

We listen to stories, in small or large groups or pairs. These are clearly difficult.

Later we return to our EWS item and begin to consider options of early warning signs that might be helpful in our own settings.

We have clarified a concept, recalled and shared school events, and now spend time together, in discussion or brainstorm, to prepare professionally for possible future storms ahead.

I Need it! I Need it!

Working as an educational consultant to Jewish schools in communities around the world entailed much travelling. Wherever I went, I had a shopping list for gifts for family members, especially children and grandchildren. Time for shopping was always short and pressured. One day a friend offered to take me to a really good toy store en route to the airport. I accepted happily and we raced off to that store so that I would have time to browse, focus and choose for the eight or nine children on that list. As we entered, a woman came in with her son, who seemed as intent as I was to see it all, concentrate and choose. In front of every single item, he began to jump up and down and scream, "I WANNIT! I WANNIT!" This was bearable once or twice but as it went on and on it became first annoying, then nerve wracking and unbearable. Finally, the mother became aware of the many unhappy looks from other shoppers and spoke to the boy. "Eppi," she said, "we cannot buy everything we see. We cannot get everything we want. We can only buy what we need." Good, I said to myself, now we can have some quiet so I can concentrate and choose... Not a second passed... Eppi began to jump up and down screaming, "I NEEDIT! I NEEDIT!"

We wonder, aloud, about questions of want and need. Is there always a clear distinction? Is it personal? Universal? Cultural?

We bridge, then, into the lesson. The set has brought us to the classic Abraham Maslow (1962) hierarchy of human needs, which will lead us to questions of the role of environments, both nurturing and destructive. This will bring us to our core questions about schools as environments. How can we make our schools healthy nurturing environments for all who live in them: students, teachers, principals?

Our story set has brought us this far...now we are ready to reflect, to recall, consider options...

We have noted the role of environment in promoting or hindering growth and our emphasis on the need for classrooms and schools to provide ongoing nurturing environments for all who live in them. Here are several set inductions we have found helpful for this issue:

Pictures

Staff members build picture collections to use in a variety of set inductions. We begin now with handing each participant a picture from a particular collection, asking them to study the picture and then share it in pairs or trios, telling each other WHAT I SEE, WHAT I FEEL. The pictures are of mother and child, children playing, couples dancing or walking or on the beach, an orchestra onstage, babies in cribs reaching out...a little girl hugging a doll. Overall feelings are of warmth, of togetherness.

Two Research Findings

We write the word "Together" on the board. Then we write "Two Stories", and begin with the classic five-year study of comparative development of two groups of children. One group lives in an orphanage, the other in a full daycare center from eight to six, picked up at night by a parent. All objective conditions are identical: diet, ratio of caretakers to children, medical team, toys, games... And, while none of the daycare children are in serious trouble, the children in the institution have a 37 percent mortality rate!! Spitz, the researcher, called this crucial life and death distinctive factor, Connectedness. More briefly, we tell of a similar study, decades after Spitz, in which the two groups studied are not children but retirees 72 years old on the average. Here too, human connections influence health and mood.

Personal Stories

Connectedness is our new word and focus. We move along to questions of our own past connections...when, where, who...Are there connections you have kept across miles, across years? Stories follow stories, sometimes a sad story of lost connection comes up, is told, responded to...

Whichever way we open, we soon move on to building, to planning how to create Connectedness in a new class, with new staff, or with new parents. We plan, re-plan, considering events, program, role-play, and much more.

Quality of Life

We created the following SET INDUCTION to introduce the topic of Effective Schooling. First, we clarify and practice the concept of Associative Thinking and rapid response. We might suggest the topic of Jerusalem and ask for the first words that come to mind, briskly and briefly (b&b in our jargon). The responses often include "Holy City", "beauty, "mountains", etc.

When the idea is clear to all, we write on the board QUALITY OF LIFE. We ask the participants to list, in writing, as many immediate thoughts as possible in one minute. This is followed by pairs sharing and combining their lists in the two minutes allotted for this exercise. Going around the circle, one member of each pair reads their list while we write their word on the board under the title. The final list includes words such as warmth, healthy environment, happiness, love, caring, family life, safety, security, and the like.

After this has been completed, we add two words in colored chalk to the title...IN SCHOOL. There is always an audible sigh in the room followed by a kind of stunned silence. The message is clear.

After a moment or two of recovery, we ask, "Is the title still suitable? What should be erased from the list? What should be added?"

Following a few brief responses, we ask the participants to discuss in pairs the following questions: "What item on the list was strongly felt in the school where I studied or taught? How did I feel it? Give examples." Several minutes later, we ask for SPECIALS, that is, "Is there something special you heard from your partner that you would like to share with the entire group?" This request often results in many moving and memorable stories.

At this point the participants are now ready to approach, study, and reflect on the educational research on Effective Schooling.

Our Client

Many years ago, the front-page picture of a local newspaper grabbed our attention, leaving us totally involved in the drama depicted. That picture became a powerful set induction for a new look at a relevant topic.

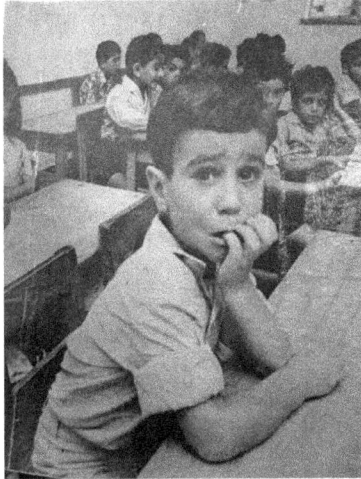

The picture shows a group of small children, six or seven years old, seated in rows in a classroom. We took this picture and mounted it on cardboard and brought it to a workshop. We opened by saying: "We are going to show a picture now and ask you to look at it carefully." We hold up the picture and walk around the room, allowing each person to take a moment to study it. We then ask, "Please write down what you **see** in this picture." They write. Then we ask, "Please write down what you **feel**." We collect all the words from the first list, they are very like each other...fear, tension, anxiety, terror, etc. no surprises....We hear their personal list of feelings....sadness, sorrow, worry. We go to the board and write: MEET OUR CLIENT. We tell them that our client was on the first page of a local newspaper the other week and the headline was The First Day of School, a real snapshot in a real classroom in our country.

From here we can develop the lesson in a variety of ways, but the core issue is clear: The emotional vulnerability of our children as they face the new school year and above all, our responsibility to create a nurturing environment - to make schools happy safe places in which to grow.

That newspaper picture was a SET INDUCTION in search of a home, a place from which it could affect and influence. Our Client has traveled the world with us, reminding all of us, professional school people, of our central mission: To serve our Client.

Miss Darcy

By chance, or perhaps not by chance, another SET INDUCTION that reached out to us was, again, a picture, this time of a small girl featured in an article in a professional journal. The article was titled *Florence Remembers*, and the author was described as a retired psychologist. We were overwhelmed by the text that accompanied the picture and it became a steady powerful SET INDUCTION throughout our work in the following decades.

MISS DARCY
Florence Wallach Freed [6]

I'm only five years old
But I can read many words
So you say I can come
To your First Grade Class
My short sturdy legs can barely
Make it up and down the
Huge Blue Bus' high steps
The big kids jeer and laugh
As I bend down to pick up my
Smooth leather pencil case
My white underpants show
But I don't care because
I'm finally going to First Grade

To Miss Darcy's Class

You are tall and beautiful
A blue-eyed Queen
Crowned with bright Red Hair
You tell me to read to all the children
Stand up straight and read out loud
Dick see Dick see Dick run
The Little Blue Dishes
Once upon a time there was a Princess

---

[6] Florence Wallach Freed is Retired Professor of Psychology, Middlesex Community College, Bedford, Massachusetts.

ORA ZOHAR

Very good reading Florence
You will sit here

First Row First Seat

That's for the Best Reader
All the other children sit
According to how well they can read
All the way up to

Sixth Row Last Seat

You also teach us Arithmetic and Penmanship
Grownup Cursive not Manuscript
You give us shiny Silver and Gold Stars
And bright Robin and Bluebird stickers
For Excellent Papers
Every morning you bestow upon us
A carton of white milk
My cup runneth over
And a chocolate-covered graham cracker
Surely goodness and mercy
You give us Recess every day
We hang gloriously upside-down
From the cold metal monkey-bars
God's In his Heaven

I love you Miss Darcy

But you are Strict
Fold your paper carefully
Or it's a Zero
No talking unless you raise your hand
No leaving the Room except at Recess
When David can't learn to read
You say he has cream cheese and sawdust
In his head I believe you

You put the Dunce Cap on Sally
You kick Jackie out for being fresh
You say Donald smells badly
And that Jane cheats
Carol is your favorite
Because she's the prettiest

FOR TEACHERS WITH LOVE

Not the smartest
And only Barbara is asked to sing
You call Bobby a Baby when he
Throws up in the middle of the
Star Spangled Banner
You say Jimmie looks like
A taxicab with its doors open
Because his ears stick out

Oh you are very Strict
But so far I am Safe in my

First Row First Seat

But I worry and worry
That I'll lose it
On Friday when you
Change the Seats
I worry so much I start
Wetting my Pants in School
I'm squirming and dying in my seat
But you won't let me
Leave the Room
Mommy gets a note from the Doctor
Please let Florence Leave the Room
Whenever she needs to
That very day you
Change all the Seats
It's only Wednesday
Not even Friday
You march me over to

Row Six Last Seat

I can't even see over the
Big Tall Boys
My little Brown Oxfords
Can't reach the floor
I'm dying of shame

You walk majestically between
Rows One and Two and say
These are the children
Who are doing very well

40

You walk ceremoniously between
Rows Three and Four and say
These are the children
Who are trying and improving

You walk cruelly between
Rows Five and Six and say
And these are the children who have
Something the Matter with Them

And I believe you

God is hiding behind the clouds
Crying millions of teardrops

I hate you Miss Darcy

You are turning into a Wicked Witch
Your red hair is burning and blazing
Like fiery Hell

Yes Miss Darcy you will
Burn Eternally in the

Last Row Last Seat

We begin the lesson by a dramatic reading of the entire text. The class is mesmerized and in total sync with the closing lines: **Yes Miss Darcy you will burn eternally in the last row last seat.**

We ask pairs to read the poem to each other, stanza by stanza. We then analyze the text together in any way at all, looking for teaching techniques used in the Darcy classroom. There are many... we note them all and then discuss them. It becomes clear that the atmosphere is toxic and the extreme change in Florence's feelings for her first grade teacher are drawn masterfully. We are not surprised by the "I Hate You" cry.

Later, or in the following session, we ask: Did you have a Miss Darcy? If so, tell us about her, or him. Many do. We note that the author is retired yet vividly recalls her first grade life. We ask if this seems reasonable. Yes, Yes, we are told, of course, this was a real trauma...and then many ancient school trauma stories come pouring out.

We consider the following situation. A colleague in your school behaves very like Miss Darcy...You see this and hear this and believe this. What should you do? There are passionate discussions...

This SET INDUCTION leads us into several rich sessions and Darcy Dimensions becomes a code clear to all.

Rules for Teachers

When we came upon this list of rules for teachers in 1872, we realized it was just too good to pass up!

Besides providing amusement for any group, the nine rules listed provide a wealth of material for serious discussions about the status of the teacher in today's society as well as the expectations that society has of its teachers. Sharing of personal experiences in pairs or threes relating to any one of the nine rules often yields amazing reports that seem to verify that, "1872 is alive and well today!"

Small and large groups can discuss the issues of expectations and status. Is today's teacher held in high esteem? Are teachers adequately paid in relation to the demands of the Board of Education, parents, principals...? Should superior teachers be rewarded? These are just a few of the questions that can be presented and discussed. Finally, for real lively action, each group can be asked to present to the large group their own list of rules for teachers in 20??

1872 RULES FOR TEACHERS

1. Teachers each day will fill lamps, clean chimneys.

2. Each teacher will bring a bucket of water and a scuttle of coal for the day's session.

3. Make your pens carefully. You may whittle nibs to the individual taste of the pupils.

4. Men teachers may take one evening each week for courting purposes, or two evenings a week if they go to church regularly.

5. After ten hours in school, the teachers may spend the remaining time reading the Bible or other good books.

6. Women teachers who marry or engage in unseemly conduct will be dismissed.

7. Every teacher should lay aside from each day pay a goodly sum of his earnings for his benefit during his declining years so that he will not become a burden on society.

8. Any teacher who smokes, uses liquor in any form, frequents pool or public halls, or gets shaved in a barber shop will give good reason to suspect his worth, intention, integrity and honesty.

9. The teacher who performs his labor faithfully and without fault for five years will be given an increase of twenty-five cents per week in his pay, providing the Board of Education approves.

OLDEST WOODEN SCHOOLHOUSE
St. Augustine, Florida

Chapter 5
FORMS – Creating Environments for
Significant Learning

In this chapter we will share many of the FORMS that we created in the Center to structure our educational processes. The FORMS, developed and implemented at the Center over the course of many years, are tools through which educators can create environments in which significant relationships and learning can develop. They have consistently supported workshop facilitators in their efforts to foster the nurturing environments in which educators could grow and mature. These educators, in turn, implemented the FORMS to create similarly nurturing environments for the children and adults in their own schools.

The FORMS improve relationships by promoting heightened personal and interpersonal awareness, and improved communication among staff. They forge organic connections between people, between material studied and the process through which it is engaged, and between the class setting and the practice setting (school). They are simple techniques, concepts or activities, easily applicable to nearly every workshop setting.

In preparing for workshops, FORMS were carefully selected for each lesson. Curricula for teacher workshops and later, for the Principals' Center, were always carefully crafted and participants became sensitive to the significance, or philosophy of our choices. Over the years, we have heard from hundreds of our graduates about how these FORMS have illuminated their professional lives.

The present chapter will describe and illustrate the basic FORMS that were present in all of our training processes. These include MENU, MISSING, HIGHIGHTS, MEMBER, JIGSAW, BACKSTAGE, and ECHOES FROM THE FIELD. A later chapter will relate to FORMS and exercises that were developed for more specific training purposes.

MENU

Definition: MENU is probably the first visible FORM in our workshops and surely the one most often used. It is a clear statement of the planned program while only hinting at what is still to come. MENU is written on the board prior to the beginning of class, with indications of emphasis or a call to pay attention to an item. Even in today's digital environment, this form has its charm. Different colored chalk and innovative questions still arouse curiosity.

Objective: MENU helps the workshop leader focus on what he wants to accomplish in each session; in the classroom, it conveys the message that the teacher has planned the lesson and is now engaging the student to consider what the upcoming hours will bring. Writing "Who's here?" on the MENU also introduces the students to each other and to the teacher – names and voices are acknowledged and the new group takes on a distinctly social flavor. In asking participants to relate why they are present, the first step in public reflective practice takes place. The group and its leader have begun to build a group culture through reflection, sharing, academic issues and personal recall. Properly used, MENU, sends a clear message of partnership to a group, and teachers learn to use it in a variety of sophisticated ways. Teachers have told us of entering their classrooms and finding MENU already partially written out by students on the board.

In Practice: An example of the menu that we use at the beginning of a new workshop is described on p. 55.

Very soon after the beginning of a workshop, teachers begin to implement MENU in their own classrooms. They soon report that MENU helps students feel included in the day's schedule and conscious of what will happen during the lesson. They like the slightly enigmatic entries on MENU and sometimes request to add an item of their own. On a different level, teachers report that MENU forces them to plan precisely what they hope to accomplish in a particular lesson, as well as how to present it clearly on the board. When MENU is on the board, it is a tool enabling teachers to remember the planned sequence, to show pupils where they are, and even to make visual alterations when necessary, demonstrating to pupils that sometimes class dynamics demand flexibility and regrouping on all parts.

MISSING

Definition: Taking attendance in every session and noting, to ourselves and to participants, which students are not in class. *In a far corner of the board, MISSING is written at the top of the board and a list is made of anyone not present.*

Objective: In a workshop, in a school setting, and throughout life in general, the sure message that someone notices whether we are present or not, and misses us, is comforting and encouraging. MISSING is an easy opportunity to express interest in a little-known other and to widen our circle of caring, thus expanding the nurturing environment in the classroom.

In Practice: The second or third time one of my classes met and the MISSING list was written on the board, a student raised her hand in protest. "What is this," she demanded, "a kindergarten class? We're all professional educators and busy adults in graduate school. If we can't make it to class, we don't expect to be publicly humiliated!" I noted the difference between *absent* and *missing*. I affirmed how important class time was, how we all valued student participation, encouraged student interaction, valued the bonding of class experiences and the opportunities to hear their questions. When a person is *missing* his absence is felt!

The following week we heard from a young man who had been on our MISSING list for two weeks. When he returned to class, he raised his hand to speak. "I've been away on reserve duty for two weeks," he said, "up north on the border. I was on patrol during the day and some nights. I was cold and muddy. But twice, on Wednesday mornings, I looked at my watch and said: 'It's Wednesday morning and far away, in Jerusalem, my classmates are looking at the board and they know that I am MISSING and they're thinking of me.'"

HIGHLIGHTS

Definition: Sharing a positive personal experience or event with workshop participants. A facilitator will cheerfully ask if anyone has had a HIGHLIGHT, a happy experience or event since our previous session.

Objective: Educators who come to our workshops are very busy people and frequently frustrated at work. When they get together, there is a tendency to focus on what is going wrong, and too rarely on what is going right. HIGHLIGHTS is critical because it invites participants to pay attention to the things in life and at work for which they are grateful, and encourages them to see the group as a place to share them. Through HIGHLIGHTS, facilitators take responsibility for seeking out the positive, highlighting it and giving it a place.

Practice: At first, the request for HIGHLIGHTS is greeted by total silence and raised eyebrows. Possibly, we may offer a very brief HIGHLIGHT of our own, such as a letter from an old friend or a family birthday celebration. Our own HIGHLIGHTS often influence what happens next – if we mention a celebration, others may also; if we bring a professional event, others may follow suit. But after a few sessions, hands go up quickly. Once in a while, either accidentally or deliberately HIGHLIGHTS does not appear on the MENU, and immediately even those who have yet to share a HIGHLIGHT will ask, "Don't we have time for HIGHLIGHTS today?"

In all the feedback that we receive at the conclusion of a series of workshops, one of the activities that participants list as "what I'll take to my class/staff" or as a significant activity is HIGHLIGHTS.

MEMBER

Definition: MEMBER is perhaps the most popular and powerful of our FORMS, where a participant in the group speaks about himself. By the third session of a new group, this FORM is introduced on the board. We choose the first candidate – someone who seems bright, confident, positive and communicative. We invite him to present himself to the group – to tell about his past, schooling, and choice of profession for seven to ten minutes. He may choose what to relate and what to omit. If he is willing to take questions from the group, the activity lasts approximately 15 minutes.

Secrecy is an important element of this FORM. Only the MEMBER of the day knows that he has been chosen, and he is usually excited and pleased to answer questions freely and openly. The audience is attentive, interested and happy to ask questions.

Objective: To remind ourselves how multi-faceted individuals are, and to share this personal richness which is often blurred in large group settings. Often, MEMBER is so powerful that we sit silently, unable to leave the room and move on to the next session. Colleagues have shared with me that students who have experienced such classes are a much more cohesive group by the following semester. No less important, is the impact that MEMBER has on the individual presenter. Many report that the week prior to the presentation is one of introspection, recall, clarification of self-image and careful selection of what to share. "I came to realize," "I suddenly understood," "pieces came together," "cause and effect emerged," "consequences and patterns became visible where there were no patterns before" – these are phrases and sentiments we hear again and again from teachers who have been MEMBER.

In Practice: Session after session groups sit spellbound while MEMBER relates the story of his life – in Israel, Yemen, South America or Russia. MEMBER notes his schooling, what led him to choose teaching and his experiences in the field. He shares his satisfactions, frustrations and hopes. Every single MEMBER is interesting, but some are unforgettable: an Arab MEMBER, who spoke of her confusion on issues of identity and loyalty; a MEMBER whose child was battling with cancer that semester and how this affected her relationship with her pupils in school; a MEMBER whose Holocaust survivor parents had sent one of their children to be reared by aunts and uncles whose own children had been killed, and the tears of rage at the loss of the brother who might have been a support while growing up as a child of survivors.

A very poignant example of the power of MEMBER took us by surprise during a ten-day seminar for teachers from abroad who came to Jerusalem for a follow-up workshop. One evening, a teacher in the group came to us in great distress. "What is it," we asked in concern, "What is wrong?" "It's R.," she told us. "She is sobbing and won't come to dinner or join any activity." Two of us, a staff member and a participant, went to investigate. R. blew her nose, took a deep breath and explained through tears: "I've never been MEMBER! Never! And in four days we go home and that will be it – no more chances for me!" This woman was in her fifties, a veteran member of her school staff, but she yearned for a different MEMBER role.

JIGSAW

Definition: The JIGSAW is a technique developed by the psychologist Elliot Aronson (2011) through which students are encouraged and enabled to engage personally and with peers with a text. Unlike the other FORMS, JIGSAW was not created by our staff but we utilized it frequently in our workshops. The activity takes time, needs space for several groups to sit together (sometimes two rooms may be needed), and can be noisy, but is well worth the effort.

Objectives: When we wanted our group to become acquainted with lengthy articles or excerpts from books, or different opinions on a topic we were studying, the JIGSAW proved to be a valuable tool. Examples of the kinds of texts we used were; Sophie Freud Loewenstein's reflections on her teaching, excerpts from Lee Iacocca's autobiography (the former chairman of Chrysler) on successful management, reflections of an Israeli Commander on leadership, or different educational views on discipline.

In Practice:

1. We divide our chosen text into four equal parts, label them A, B, C, and D, and distribute one part to each of the participants for silent reading. We sometimes suggest writing notes for easier discussion later on. Timing depends on the difficulty or complexity of the texts.

2. Participants then sit in homogeneous groups of four; A's, B's, C's and D's together. Each group discusses the text and writes a short précis or summary together, each individual having the same précis. In a classroom situation, this is especially advantageous for weaker students. The teacher in advance can assure that there will always be stronger students in every homogeneous group. Every member of the group will understand and be prepared to teach his part!

3. Participants now form new heterogeneous groups with representatives from A, B, C, and D. In turn, each member reads his précis followed by a discussion of the main ideas.

4. At this point, there are two possibilities. Members are asked to reread their original texts and underline **one** sentence that

has special significance for them, positively or negatively. In their small groups, members in turn read their sentences and briefly explain why they chose that sentence. An alternative is for everyone to return to the original large circle or group with their underlined sentences in hand. Going in turn around the room, each member reads his chosen sentence with **no** comments from the rest of the group. This is often a powerful and moving closure to the activity.

Often at the close of such an activity, the workshop leader will ask for reactions to the activity itself. This generally leads to a thorough analysis of the activity with all its advantages for classroom use and the possible difficulties that might arise.

BACKSTAGE

Definition: BACKSTAGE is the review and analysis of the step-by-step process of our workshop hours together. We invite participants to go back to the MENU and with its help to recall with us what had taken place in the workshop. Looking at each activity, we share with them what we had planned and why, what options we faced as the process progressed, and why we made particular choices. We consider whether any of these teaching strategies could be transferable to their classrooms and invite them to try them out.

Objective: BACKSTAGE takes workshop participants into our professional confidence by clarifying what we have attempted to build together. By reflecting jointly with them about our own decisions and how we made them we enable them to understand more deeply the reflective processes that underlie successful teaching, thereby developing their capacity to work reflectively in their own contexts.

In Practice: Through BACKSTAGE, participants are given an invaluable opportunity to learn that successful teaching requires a combination of very precise and goal-focused planning and a capacity for flexibility in response to a developing process. Participants frequently reported taking the strategies to design lessons with their own students, or to prepare faculty meetings.

ECHOES FROM THE FIELD

Definition: ECHOES FROM THE FIELD are reports of applying an aspect of the workshop in the classroom or school life during the time since the last meeting. Participants are asked to take one or two workshop activities into their own classroom and to relate the experience to us. We ask if anyone has felt any ECHOES; sometimes no one has. We ask again the following session. Eventually, in every group, someone brings an ECHO. There is great pleasure in listening to the wonderfully reflective reporting as participants describe what they did and share their questions and answers.

Objective: The objectives here are two-fold: To gain insight into and reinforce the process of internalization taking place among participants; and to encourage participants to import new ideas into their classes. In addition, teachers are aware that if it works, they will get positive reinforcement in the next session. If it is not successful, they will have the opportunity to present the experience to the group for analysis and practical improvements.

In Practice: In a workshop for kindergarten teachers, one of the members reported on how she used the JIGSAW effectively in her kindergarten class for teaching about citrus fruits. The "text" was an orange, grapefruit, clementine or lemon. In their homogeneous groups, the children were asked to describe their fruit noting its color, smell, size etc. In the mixed group, each member described his fruit, and the group was then asked to define the similarities and differences between all the citrus fruits!

Some of the most rewarding ECHOES relate how classroom teachers of all grade levels have introduced MEMBER into their classrooms. Teachers apply MEMBER in creative ways – for bonding and for solving specific social situations (e.g., including new immigrant children, integrating children from different feeder schools, etc.). Teachers tell about asking the principal, school nurse or librarian to be MEMBER, and of the weekly excitement before the class learns who MEMBER is.

The following ECHO was shared by a creative and reflective young *Mechanechet* of a 12th grade class who was a student in my graduate seminar. She was upset about a festering situation between her class and their physics teacher, a new immigrant from the former Soviet Union. She described a recent crisis in which the physics teacher arrived at the classroom door after the bell had sounded. Pupils had not yet responded to the bell and the energetic noise of recess still raged.

A student who had gone out to the hallway saw the physics teacher.

"Come in," says the pupil, "we're all inside."

"No," says Teacher, "I cannot come in until you are all standing."

"What?" says pupil, "Why should we all stand?"

"Because," answers Teacher, "in Russia all pupils stand up when Teacher comes into the classroom."

"Well!" says the 12th grader. "This is not Russia, and in Israel we do not stand for teachers, so you may as well come in."

"No", says Teacher, "I will not enter."

For the next class meeting, my graduate student invited the physics teacher to come as MEMBER. She explained the FORM to him, reviewing his role and reminding him of the secrecy and surprise involved. He was happy to arrive and speak. The pupils sat in stunned silence as he told of his life, his arrest and his years as a *Refusenik*[7] in faraway Russia. With tears of joy in his eyes, he ended: "Here I am at last, in the land of Israel, teaching wonderful Jewish children!" After class, the pupils reluctantly grumbled to the teacher: "How could you do that to us! Now we'll never be able to make trouble for him again!"

And they never did.

---

[7] Refusenik - an unofficial term for individuals, typically but not exclusively Soviet Jews, who were denied permission to emigrate abroad by the authorities of the former Soviet Union and other countries of the Eastern bloc.

Chapter 6
The Staff Development Workshop

Throughout the years, I have learned much about teachers, both when they taught my own children, and even now as they teach my grandchildren. There have been teachers who helped them to grow, and teachers who blocked growth. There have been teachers who encouraged us to be partners in the educational journey and those who made us into adversaries. I believe that the single element in a school year that determines joy or misery, is the teacher's attitude, behavior, and basic philosophy of life. I acknowledge Maslow's (1962) perception that human growth is dependent on environment, which is either nurturing or crippling, but never neutral. Similarly, schools must be consciously nurturing. If they are not, they will be negative or destructive, never merely neutral.

For each child, the school environment is created mostly by his teachers. Accordingly, in our Center's staff development workshops throughout Israel and other parts of the world, we reached out to teachers to give them the vision, the courage, and the tools to create nurturing school environments. In this chapter, we describe the format and structure of these staff development workshops, and then provide several illustrations of the model in action.

Workshop Format

The teacher workshops of the Center's first decade had a classic format: biweekly workshops held at the school, in whatever room or comfortable space was available, preferably with coffee facilities. Each session lasted approximately four hours, beginning at noon, as teachers were in class all morning and remained after hours for the workshop. The school would arrange grade-wide or school-wide activities to coincide with these meetings in order to minimize lost teaching hours.

The program generally spanned 15 sessions, accompanying the group throughout the entire school year.

Workshop Structure

The workshops generally followed principles common to settings for individuals in the helping professions: exploration of self, understanding of self, and changing of self on the basis of that understanding. In practice, workshop leaders established a strong support environment designed to help participants feel nurtured, trusting and receptive to others. This bottom line atmosphere was essential if teachers were to accept the challenges of professional self-assessment and growth.

Participants spent approximately 65 percent of workshop time on a common curriculum of topics, texts and activities. All groups contended with role definitions, goal clarifications, formulation of appropriate objectives, partnerships with colleagues and homes, motivation, teacher stress, learning styles, leadership styles and relevant research on effective schools. As groups became more cohesive and supportive, members brought in their own agendas: their personal difficulties with classroom management; specific crises with pupils, colleagues or administrators; personal symptoms of burnout and fatigue; and requests for advice and help from the entire group. These agendas, unique to each workshop group, generated the other 35 percent of the program.

The Group as Resource

Each group also became a resource to its members, while leaders modeled the roles of facilitator, craftsperson and teacher. They used a wide variety of teaching techniques. Each session involved participants in an integrated program of substance and style, while BACKSTAGE analyses of structured activities helped to apply particular issues or techniques to individual professional contexts.

During the two weeks between sessions, teachers were asked to reflect, to apply an activity or theme to their own context and to internalize what they had learned. This combination of intensive academic study followed by a two-week interval was designed to accompany workshop participants on their journey through the school year, thereby maximizing impact.

The Model in Action: The First Session

How do we launch a new workshop for a group of teachers we have never met? We begin by writing today's MENU on the board, always following the same structure:

1. Hello, Who's Here?

2. Two Questions

3. Pictures

4. The Search

5. Looking Ahead

After the obvious social nature of the first item, we ask participants to prepare paper and pencil and to be ready to answer two questions in writing, privately. The answer to each is a number. We wait until all are ready and curious. The first question is presented: "How many teachers have you had in your life?" We note that we refer only to professional teachers, although for many of us our parents and extended family were possibly our truest teachers. Familiar questions arise: From what age? Do we really mean all their student lives? Are university faculty considered teachers?

We clarify that we are looking for a concrete answer, which may vary in quantity considerably, depending upon personal experience. Inevitably, a great sigh is heard and then silence, as each person recalls, calculates and finally writes a number.

We write each number on the board in blue marker, going around the room in order. The numbers range from 50 to 200, depending on levels of schooling and the country of schooling.

We look at the numbers and present the second question: "For each of you personally, how many of these teachers were Good Teachers?" A few voices will call out, "What do you mean by Good Teachers?" Our response is always the same: "Whomever **you** consider to be a good teacher!" Acceptance, silence, thoughtful faces. We wait. When their answers are ready, we circle the room again, in the same order, and in pink marker write each person's second answer next to his first. As the pink list grows, even before we get to finish hearing from everyone, there is an audible feeling of tension in the room. When we complete the pink list alongside the blue list, the picture becomes amazingly clear. The blackboard speaks for itself! The pink numbers are just a fraction of their corresponding blue numbers!

Before commenting, we let the message sink in as the room fills with discomfort and even shock. After a few minutes of their reactions, the only comment that we make is that this list on the board is universal. In **all** our workshops, whether with kindergarten teachers or university lecturers, in Israel and abroad, the overwhelming account is the same; the Good Teacher list is about 20 percent of the Teachers in My Life list. In other words, good teachers are rare! And all of us sitting here hope that someday when our pupils are asked the same questions, they will define us as "pink" teachers!

When we feel the initial tension has abated, we once again turn to our participants and ask them, quietly, to think of three teachers on their pink list and write their names. Recalling their names helps to focus on particular teachers. We ask them to list their characteristics next to their names. This exercise changes the atmosphere in the room; the nostalgic recall of their good teachers brings smiles to their faces as they write eagerly. When we feel they have pretty much concluded, we ask them to choose **one** of the three teachers and share their description with their immediate neighbor, each one taking two minutes to talk about this **good** teacher. A hum of pleasantness fills the room, but we have to stop each one after two minutes and give the neighbor equal time to share.

We then ask each participant to read **one** characteristic from his list, and this is written on the board by the workshop leader, not haphazardly but carefully in two lists. Characteristics such as "caring", "sensitivity", "encouraging" will go on one list while other characteristics such as "knew how to impart the material", "aroused curiosity", "exciting lessons", were listed separately. These two lists express two different approaches to teaching: Carl Rogers' approach of

Teaching as Facilitating and Dwight Allen's approach of Teaching as Craft.

We explain in a few sentences the differences between these two approaches. Then we express the Center's conviction that Good Teaching comprises the combination of **both** as we sketch a big heart around the two lists.

Now we are ready to begin!

BACKSTAGE: What have we tried to do in this first session? Initially, we have tried to establish an informal social tone through usage of Hello and Who's Here, where we learn names and roles held in the school. Undoubtedly, however, it is the two questions and the follow-up activities that are the heart of the session. We use the personal school experience of people in the room to force ourselves as professionals to reflect on the reality of our collective past and its multiple meanings. A slight shift is made, from the defensive teacher stance in the face of suggested change, to identification with our pupil-selves in long ago classrooms, possibly leading to empathy for pupils we know and teach today. During this session, we have thought, listened, shared and learned – about ourselves and each other, about teachers elsewhere in the world and about research findings. A bold statement about the teaching profession has been made today. We recognize that this year and this framework are an invitation to modify the statement, together.

The Model in Action: The Second Session

In the following session, workshops may begin moving in different directions, but certain points will be shared by all. A review of the first session will take place as pairs of participants relate any one idea or experience that they recall or consider important. Questions or thoughts about that session will be discussed. A new unit from our classic curriculum will be shared, with opportunities to raise issues that participants would like to present to the group. Toward the end of this session, BACKSTAGE, one of the most important of our workshop FORMS, will be introduced.

Overview

During the course of our workshops, teachers begin to note the four dimensions inherent in our studying about teaching:

1. Experiential – including all the actual events of the workshop.

2. Academic – especially the research findings on Good Teachers in early sessions and the shift to the search for Good Teaching.

3. Analytic – revolves around the diversified BACKSTAGE exercises.

4. Didactic – relates to the many ways we consider taking home elements of that experience.

Sometimes we ask paired participants to tell each other why they have not brought any ECHOES, or to discuss what ECHO they would have liked to bring. Listing reasons for not bringing ECHOES could follow, an activity valuable for all. Possibilities range from not feeling an activity is appropriate to the class, not feeling comfortable introducing a new style, to fear of pupils' rejection of a new activity. Sometimes a teacher will report about an ECHO that did not work, and we deliberate together. Session leads to session and we travel the school year together, bringing HIGHLIGHTS, ECHOES and REQUESTS from participants as we build on research studies and theories. We recall long-ago issues such as teacher favoritism or test anxiety and meditate on how these feature in our own classrooms today. We change perspectives constantly, from "me" as pupil to "me" as teacher. We clarify, empathize, think and balance – in a word, we reflect on our own professional practice. By midyear, after five sessions, each workshop will be operative as a supportive professional environment for its participants, supportive enough to air personal concerns and requests for help.

REQUESTS vary greatly and range from help with disciplinary strategies, or anxiety about professional burnout, to intensely personal concerns such as a conflict with a parent or colleague. The clear responsibility of the workshop leaders is to create and maintain a group culture of respect, acceptance, support and growth. Above and beyond particular topics addressed throughout the year, what is especially important is the development of a staff room in which members of different disciplines know each other both personally and professionally.

Feedback from Participants

Consistent feedback was received from numerous participants over the years. Participants repeatedly indicated that they had gained knowledge, taken home new techniques, changed their attitudes, formed new friendships, changed the character of their relationship with other staff members, and had their personal batteries recharged. Above all, they reported having developed a profound sense of significance in their lives and a renewed commitment to invest in their profession. Below are a number of representative quotes from written feedback provided by teachers at the conclusion of school workshops.

- *The workshops are an important resource for me as a teacher. I learned to understand the pupils and to make their lives in school less of a burden and more of a joy.*

- *The workshops provided us with a lot of new information and helped us learn new didactic methods. In addition, they helped us analyze problems that we had to deal with in our everyday work.*

- *I learned how to give the children the love they deserve…*

- *I was able to reflect on my own teaching styles and better understand how to connect with children.*

- *As the workshop progressed I came to understand what you meant by "connectedness". You opened up a whole new world for me. The workshop has put a permanent stamp on who I am as an educator and for that I am eternally grateful.*

- *The workshops contribute a lot to bringing the teachers in the school closer to one another and to improving the status of the teachers.*

- *Being students once again after so many years brought us closer to our students.*

- *I changed the way I relate to the students. I changed and improved my teaching methods. I improved my relations with the other teachers…I found new ways to deal with my students' problems. I deal differently now with problems in the classroom. The class has an improved image.*

Behind the Scenes with Staff of a Workshop – Aviva Pinchuk

Approximately 25 staff members worked at the National Center for Staff Development and the Principals' Center. The group was a diverse cross section of Israeli society in outlook, way of life, family backgrounds, political views and ideology. There was a mix of male and female, religious and secular, from kibbutzim, rural communities and cities throughout Israel. In addition, there were immigrants from all parts of the world as well as Israeli-born citizens. There were grandparents, young parents and singles. All came from the World of Teaching and shared similar educational and moral values. In biweekly staff meetings under the directorship of Dr. Ora Zohar, we learned to accept and respect the differences in each other, a goal we aimed for in the workshops we conducted.

Staff meetings consisted of reports and analyses of the many workshops given throughout the country. Ora always introduced the latest research in education, generating lively discussions and ideas of how to transfer these findings to our workshops. Activities were conducted just as our workshops were, sitting in a circle, sharing, listening, responding, and exchanging views and experiences in pairs, small groups or full group discussions. Our meetings were always spiced with SHRT (Systematic Humanistic Relationship Training) exercises that created a nurturing environment of flexibility, empathy, acceptance and respect.

One of the basic principles of the Center was that all workshops were conducted by paired staff members, modeling peer teaching. This method also provided workshop participants with an added sense of interest as they were exposed to variations in appearance, voice, intonation, language and accent. What follows is the behind-the-scenes how-to of two staff members planning and processing a workshop:

Stage One: Pre-Workshop Planning

Whenever possible, the first step in planning a workshop was to meet with the principal to learn about the school and the teaching staff and to clarify the principal's goals and expectations of the workshop. With this vital information in hand, the co-facilitators would begin to map out the workshops in detail. Planning had to take into consideration not only the principal's expectations, but also the nature and needs of the participants. Besides content, the format was of utmost importance –

methodology, techniques and timing were essential for the success of the workshop. Through our discussions and exchange of ideas and opinions, we learned to understand each other and to recognize our individual strengths. These discussions and debates broadened our minds and ignited sparks of creativity – *A knife can be sharpened only against the edge of another knife* (an ancient Jewish proverb).

In our preparation sessions, we always simulated and role-played what we expected our participants to experience, followed by mutual feedback, which provided valuable tools for successful planning. The plan for a four-hour workshop thus completed, we then divided the program in such a way that each of us had an equal role, usually with one opening and the other closing.

Although every minute of the workshop was carefully planned, including the breaks, we nonetheless approached each workshop with great apprehension and trepidation. Had we considered everything? Will we be stepping on someone's toes? Is there a Pandora's Box waiting on the sidelines? Will they find the material relevant? Will we be able to hold their interest for so many hours? Will they like us and come back for more? Or will they feel we're wasting their time? It was always comforting to know that we had each other!

Stage Two: The Workshop

We worked in pairs, but throughout the workshop, we never had a moment's rest! When one was directing, the partner would be observing the participants and jotting down notes, or updating a latecomer or facilitating a small group discussion. During pair sharing or small group discussions, we would exchange observations or decide on sudden changes in the plan. Even coffee breaks were used for fine-tuning the remainder of the program, giving each other feedback, and initiating conversation with individual participants. Sometimes we even had time to drink our coffee!

Stage Three: Post-Mortem

The post-mortem commenced immediately after the last participant left the room. We would look at each other and then…. Clap our hands in delight, breathe a sigh of relief, or wring our hands in worry. It was amazing how we were always "in sync" in our initial reaction! If we felt it was not a particularly successful workshop we would give it a grade from 1 to 10. It was always so encouraging to hear your partner give it a higher grade than you!

On the way home, whether by car, bus, or plane, we would begin the dissection of the workshop. We asked ourselves how we rated the effectiveness of our planning: Were the topics and activities relevant? Did we complete the program as planned? If not, why not? Was our timing satisfactory? What did we learn from the reactions of the participants? Were there participants who needed special attention? Did our participants leave with a sense of accomplishment; that their time was well spent? How did we feel this? How can we integrate their requests into the planning of our next workshop with them? We were also concerned about the technical aspects that could contribute to or detract from the effectiveness of the workshop, such as the comfort of the seats and the room, and the adequacy of the lighting, ventilation, and refreshments.

In their written feedback submitted at the conclusion of the series of workshops, the participants often commented on the fact that we worked as a pair. Common remarks were, "The coordination between the two of you was remarkable!" And, "You were two people who functioned as one."

Story from the Field, by Shoshana Tessler and Aviva Pinchuk

We were asked by a Jerusalem school to conduct four workshops concentrating on Staff Cooperation and Development. We were not forewarned of the tense atmosphere among the staff and between the staff and the principal. To our absolute shock, the festering wound burst immediately in our faces! At the first opportunity to talk freely, the teachers complained bitterly of an authoritarian principal and animosity between the teachers on the staff. In addition, the senior teachers felt totally unappreciated. The frustration and anger expressed was so great, we both felt under attack! A new teacher was visibly upset because she was not aware that any of this existed! What did she fall into?

We thought: "What did **we** fall into?" "What damage have we done? How can we fix it?"

Our stress tolerance was excellent – we had been trained well – and our original plan went out the window. We had to address the emotions exploding in the room. At the conclusion of our four sessions with them, many expressed the desire to continue. We were surrounded by teachers who were visibly angry but felt that we behaved "honorably."

In our post-mortem later, Shoshana and I disagreed. I felt they had aired their dirty laundry in public; it was painful and visibly embarrassing for them. Shoshana was more inclined to continue if possible. For me, it was so unpleasant I just didn't want to go back.

Three Months Later

At the Conference of Israeli English Teachers in Jerusalem, I spotted M., an English teacher at the school. After some friendly exchanges she suddenly offered, "You know, after you and Shoshana left something happened. One of the points of bitterness amongst the staff was the fact that the principal always dictated who would be excused from the classroom to attend workshops. There was a lot of resentment and jealousy among those who were not selected to attend. As a result of discussing these feelings openly in one of the sessions, a few of the teachers approached the principal – something they had never done before! The principal reacted very positively and willingly agreed to open up all the in-service opportunities. That all came about because of your workshop," she said.

M. continued, "After your workshops, something snapped. It really made a difference. Everyone is so much happier. There was a school trip and everyone came even though they didn't have to. They came for the **social** part. One of the teachers who was affected the most is Y (one of the oldest-about-to-retire teachers who spoke very bitterly about her feeling of being made to feel she had outlived her usefulness). She dresses nicely now. She even organized a lovely graduation party. She comes to school so much happier."

After I recovered from the initial shock of this unexpected feedback, I asked M. to what she attributed the changes. "I think the fact that everyone had a chance to talk about their feelings instead of boiling inside all the time. People are much happier."

To M.'s great astonishment, I was greatly moved by this brief encounter. I told her how Shoshana and I had had mixed feelings (to put it mildly) about the kind of workshop we gave and how her feedback adds a whole new dimension to my thoughts.

Only a few minutes passed between my initial casual hello to M. and an emotional good-bye. Her few sentences left such a stirring impact on me and I was still reeling hours later. Never before had we gotten such strong results in such a short time.

This episode confirms my view that there is always room for hope and optimism; there's always good to be had even from something unpleasant and painful. Sometimes we have to wait for it to become apparent.

The Druze Experience: The Teachers' Workshop in Usfia - Chava Zohar

Usfia is one of the larger Druze communities in Israel located on Mount Carmel. Education is of utmost importance in Usfia as it serves as a vital means of preserving the Druze religion, tradition and culture. For this reason, the Principal of the main school there, Farouk, registered for the two-year course of the Principals' Center.

As a result of his participation in that course, Farouk was convinced that this model of in-service training could be beneficial to his teaching staff. Furthermore, in his initial meeting with us, Farouk stressed that the parent body puts high demands on the school, wishing to see more of their children graduate high school and eventually proceed to academic studies. He believed the workshops could be an intellectual professional experience as well as a trigger for more staff cohesiveness and collegiality. The ultimate result in his view would be better teaching!

And so, in October 1991, my co-facilitator and I found ourselves making our way up north to Usfia by bus and taxi. We were delighted to find that we could learn a good deal about the social, religious, and political realities from our friendly driver. For example, we learned that there is remarkable diversity in the Druze community, which might reflect itself during the workshop sessions. And it did.

The Druze life style and culture is so different from ours and yet it became clear that their issues and problems are the same as for teachers all over the world! Below is a small sampling of some of the

Druze teachers' requests that could be any teaching staff's anywhere in the world.

- What is the most effective way of enforcing discipline?

- Should teachers stay with the same class from year to year? Should this be school policy or left up to the individual teacher?

- How should a teacher handle an unplanned visit of the principal to the classroom?

- What tools can a teacher acquire to handle problematic meetings with parents? Pupils? Colleagues?

The last meeting of that year was a special highlight for all of us. The whole group traveled to Jerusalem to visit the Center on the campus of Hebrew University on Mount Scopus. They met with the entire staff of the Center and were treated to a special workshop with Ora Zohar, a session at the video studio where they practiced observation of themselves and each other, and a tour of the campus including time for journal reading in the Library of Education. For the finale, the whole group came to my home for a light meal and to discuss the day's experience.

We departed with warm wishes while looking forward to a second year of joint efforts to continue what had been started in Usifya!

Chapter 7
Principals and the Principals' Center

The Principals' Center: Beginnings

By 1986 we had worked with approximately 500 school professionals each year over a period of eight years in a variety of roles and settings. The same basic convictions were the foundations of the model for each training, and created the particular culture unique to the Center's work. Over these years, we were attentive to the voices of principals with whom we had worked closely – from Petah Tikva and Tiberius, from Kiryat Shmona and Beersheba, from Liverpool and London. Though the language and location differed, the statements were remarkably similar. Many principals had told us how rarely they had time for thought and reflection, for clarification of their own vision for their school and for consideration of strategies to bring themselves and their staff closer to that vision. Principals shared their sense of drowning in administrative demands, and spoke of the pressures of daily maintenance and emergencies that filled their hours and drained their energies.

As our workshops grew, principals of participating staffs began to hear of studies and ideas from their teachers. They began to turn to us and ask, "What about us? Don't we need to learn, to know more about up-to-date educational trends and findings in the world?" So we considered inviting the principals to become part of their in-house study group. Workshop participants shot down this idea fiercely. "No, no!" they begged. "That will spoil what we have here, a truly confidential forum for anything we want to bring up about our problems, difficulties, anxieties or complaints."

We identified deeply felt needs not being met. There was a need to learn more of what was known in the world about school leadership, to develop personal strengths and to explore ways of compensating for areas of personal weakness. There was a need to gain a wider range of competencies as well as a need to think, to reconsider priorities and re-examine positions and policies long held.

All of the voices spoke of the essential loneliness of the role and the lack of a peer group of other principals, a forum where ideas could be crystallized, concerns aired and failures acknowledged and reflected upon. Heads of schools, responsible for the nurturing of pupils and staff, often felt the lack of a personal/professional nurturing environment that would enable them to advance toward self-realization.

Our Center's experience in the field consistently confirmed the centrality of the principal in the overall effectiveness of each school and in the climate of the school for both staff and pupils. Clearly, the Center could not meet the deepest challenges of education without developing a context in which we could systematically engage principals and provide them with the type of experiences we had been providing their teachers.

🍎 🍎 🍎

An old folktale tells of a famous Maggid *(itinerant preacher) who arrived in town and immediately asked the wealthy leader of the community for ten rubles.*

"Ten rubles!" gasped the rich man. "We have not discussed a fee at all... and surely – speakers are paid after the talk and not before."

The Maggid *was adamant and ten rubles changed pockets. After his brilliant talk, received enthusiastically by the townspeople, the* Maggid *returned the money to the rich man.*

"I am doubly confused," said he. "You demanded money before you spoke and now return the entire sum untouched. Of what use was it to you then?"

"Ah," smiled the Maggid, *"of use beyond description – for I cannot begin to describe the difference it makes to the speaker when there are ten rubles in his pocket."*

🍎 🍎 🍎

The enormity of this truth was borne out to me by experiences confirming that there may be both short and long-term effects of rubles in the pocket. As Director of the struggling Center, I was always hoping for a miracle that would provide financial support. In 1986, I met a generous contributor to many causes in Israel and vividly described the Center's work and budgetary struggles. The Donor, as he at once became known in my mind, listened thoughtfully and said that his fund would not support ongoing work but would consider funding a new undertaking at my initiative.

This was the opportunity to invest in the professional growth of school principals by establishing a Principals' Center at the School of Education of the Hebrew University. The Principals' Center would offer seminars in educational leadership, structured opportunities for study and work and time for thoughtful discussion with colleagues.

In the best *Maggid* tradition, I initiated simultaneous dialogues with the Ministry of Education, the national unions of primary and secondary principals, a number of principals in the field and the University and Center staff. A steering committee with representatives of each body was launched and policy questions were considered while the Center staff began building the actual course of study.

The proposed model was a two-year program, where groups would meet three times a year for a three-day period in a residential setting. The Principals' Center would be national and composed of two separate groups – primary and secondary school principals. Participants would be asked to pay an annual membership fee of $100. The Ministry undertook to publicize the new Center, to help in recruitment and interviewing, to allow participating principals nine days off during the school year and to credit program graduates with salary increments. The University would co-sponsor the Principals' Center with the Ministry, adding the considerable prestige of its name to the project. And the Center staff, with input from a core of colleagues who were principals, would design and lead the actual seminars.

Everyone was pleased, since helping principals to develop professionally is a worthwhile endeavor and no less important – for a Ministry and University beset with financial worries – was the fact that the Donor was paying all the bills. Many people warned us that Israeli principals would not respond to our publicized approach of "peer forums, time for thoughtful discussion, exploration of personal-professional goals," etc. It was not, they told us, sufficiently "nuts and bolts", and did not even offer a detailed list of topics, speakers or events. They predicted that practical-minded administrators would not buy this product.

Privately, we agreed that if 15 appropriate candidates materialized we would open one group. Meanwhile Center staff went into high gear: reading, researching studies for school principals, preparing materials and organizing residence and study rooms. In the midst of this excitement the unbelievable happened – the Donor disappeared. His foundation sent a warm letter of regret and wished us good luck.

The rubles in our pocket had carried us through months of negotiation, persuasion and planning. Penniless again, Center staff met secretly to consider the crisis. To lose the momentum gained during the past six months of work would mean a serious setback for the dream of a Principals' Center, possibly to be lost forever. We decided unanimously to carry on exactly as if we still had a Donor. We agreed to volunteer our services and to take on extra work abroad to earn enough to subsidize the new project. In effect, we became the Donor. We shared none of this with any of our partners and forged ahead, hoping for candidates. One hundred and twenty seven principals applied – we were overwhelmed and validated.

We learned valuable lessons. The *Maggid* was right about the power of money in the pocket, for the Donor factor was a catalyst for creative thinking and intensive action. But we learned another lesson too: that a small group of educators committed to a vision can, against all odds, create new realities.

The Principals' Center operated from 1986 until 2007, training 16 cohorts of Israeli principals from throughout the country and from all sectors of Israeli society. Center staff also traveled abroad and trained groups of principals from Jewish schools throughout the world, including South Africa, Toronto, Great Britain, Mexico and Australia. Finally, Palestinian principals from Gaza and from the West Bank also benefited from training in the early 1990s following the Oslo accords.

Adaptation of the Center Model

As we planned to open this new chapter in our work, the Principals' Center, we came to realize that certain changes would be helpful and, in fact, essential. As always, there were four elements to take into consideration: Format, FORMS, Culture and Curriculum.

Format

One basic change would be the format or schedule of group meetings. Our workshops had usually met once in two weeks in the school building of the staff involved. Clearly, as the principals were coming from all over the country, a central venue would be needed. Additionally, as participants had to travel to sessions, a new timetable became necessary. We decided to hold meetings three times a year in a residential setting that would allow maximum hours of study with minimum travel time. We were determined that these hours would not take place during school vacation days but rather be clearly recognized as an integral part of a principal's professional life. The Ministry of Education agreed to our plan and also agreed to recognize Center study days as official in-service credits which meant, in the long run, a small increment of salary.

We decided to meet in Beit Meirsdorf, the faculty club and hotel of the Mt Scopus campus of Hebrew University in Jerusalem. This was excellent for several reasons. Firstly, the physical setting is stunning with a panoramic view of the city and surroundings. Secondly, the halls are bustling with crowds of students and faculty, giving us a background of academic life and highlighting the academic credibility of our program. And finally, for each of the participants, coming to Jerusalem had an added spiritual historic dimension.

The fact that there were a specific limited number of rooms obviously limited the size of the groups we could invite, but this was actually to our advantage. Thus, we opened the Center with 40 principals in two groups of 20, and met for three days in early fall, mid-winter and finally late spring. This proved an excellent decision, providing a powerfully effective format.

FORMS and Culture

All the FORMS used in our workshops were both appropriate and effective with our new participants. This was also true of the Culture of our work. One popular definition of culture is, "That's the way we do things around here," and thus as we moved with MENU and MEMBER and many of our FORMS, the unique culture of our Center moved with us. This was brought home to us from time to time as one new participant or another would echo earlier comments such as, "What is this, a summer camp?" Or, "Do you realize where we all live?" Happily for all, these same critics became allies and friends as they adjusted to the newness of the Culture and were taken BACKSTAGE to reflect with us on the **why** of how we worked.

Curriculum

Like the Format, the Curriculum for Principals, built on the basic convictions, had to be significantly different from that of teachers. To a great extent the topics used in teacher sessions were appropriate to principals as well. Nevertheless, we also needed to develop new units specifically for principals. These units included: work in our lives, the role of the workplace in our satisfaction or dissatisfaction, building a team, sharing power and decision-making, styles of leadership, areas of school/community cooperation, school and parents, principal as role model for staff, systematic observation of teaching and productive feedback to teachers, supervision of staff, attending and validating.

Below is a brief description of how we approached the topic of Leadership.

SET INDUCTION

> A rumor reached one of the towns in Poland that on the following day the first train would arrive.

> All of the town's people dressed up in their Sabbath clothes and came out to observe the new wonder. Among them was the famous Hassidic rabbi and leader who lived there.

> The Rabbi did not suffice himself with looking at the train. He went up to it to feel the cars and the engine with his own hands. His followers wondered at the meaning of their rabbi's actions, and they asked him about it.

> He replied: Everything in the world has something to teach us. I saw the train and noticed that the cars were cold as frost, but the

locomotive was burning hot. From this, I learned that a leader who is hot and burning with passion has the power to pull even the many who are ice-cold!

With this charming story as our SET INDUCTION we open the topic of Leadership in the Principals' Center. Using texts from educational or business leadership journals or personal pieces (such as Lee Iacocca's autobiography or excerpts from a book about exceptional military leaders) we set the stage for analysis of the qualities of Good Leadership. We suggest choosing three or four short texts to be studied JIGSAW style or through individual reading and sharing. We then ask our participants to list the Qualities of Leadership evident in these texts. These can be listed on the board.

We then invite personal responses by having groups of **three** tell about a person that they knew/know who exemplifies one or more of these Leadership qualities.

Thomas Sergiovanni (1996) discusses what he calls the Five Forces of Leadership in order of importance for excellence in Leadership. We distribute Sergiovanni's table of the first **three** Forces (in his words: Technical, Human, and Educational) which describes the theoretical constructs and the links to Excellence of each force. These are the basic Leadership qualities that "keep the train going." Groups of three or five study the table together and each member chooses and shares **one** he feels is his strength and **one** which he would like to improve.

We then distribute Sergiovanni's table of Forces Four and Five which he calls the Symbolic and Cultural Forces, or using Sergiovanni's metaphors, the forces that transform the principal into a "Chief" or "High Priest," respectively. "The presence [of these two forces] is essential to excellence in schooling..." In the words of the Chassidic Leader, these are the forces which provide the intense heat for the locomotive providing the energy to pull along the cold cars!

The whole group can then be asked if some members would like to share a personal story of a "Chief" or "High Priest" they knew, as a pupil, student, staff member...By then, the members are ready to reflect and suggest ways for principals to not only function as "good" principals but to become charismatic and effective Leaders of their communities.

With so much responsibility given to us for our children's future, we dare not miss the train!

INBOX

One of the graduates of our Principals' Center, who later became a group leader himself in the Center, remarked on the relevance and significance of one of the many activities designed for principals, the INBOX. [8]

Center staff learned about this exercise from David Leopard, who at the time directed the National Assessment Center for High School Principals in the United States. It is designed to help principals analyze how and why they make certain decisions, thus enabling them to prioritize and improve their decision-making skills. The workshop leader opens the activity by articulating the fact that principals must make many decisions every day, including difficult, urgent, and long reaching ones.

The INBOX exercise simulates a real life situation for the principal. Upon entering his office in the morning, the Principal often finds a pile of letters, memos and notes on his desk, in his INBOX. Besides dealing with the regular pressures of the school day, the Principal must also read, analyze and prioritize the written material on his desk. He has very little time to decide which items need immediate attention and which can wait.

In this exercise, each principal receives an INBOX containing about 12 letters/memos reflecting real school life situations. Below are some examples of the contents of the INBOX:

- a letter from the Supervisor asking for the results of the nationwide arithmetic exams;

- a note from the gymnastics teacher reporting on flooding in the gym;

- a memo from the teachers who prepared a special reading comprehension curriculum for first to third graders asking the principal for his response;

- a letter from a potential donor asking for a meeting with the principal;

---

[8] This exercise pre-dated the prevalence of the e-mail "Inbox," but the principles remain the same.

- a note from a teacher informing the principal of a girl who had a sudden asthma attack and needs immediate medical attention;

- a note from a teacher informing him that due to her pregnancy she must go on immediate bed rest and will be absent from school for a few months;

- a letter from a teacher asking the principal to approve the budget for a special school wide project.

The principals are then asked to work individually. They are given one hour to read the letters, prioritize, respond and be prepared to explain their reasons for all their decisions and reactions to these letters. The following questions for individual thinking are posed:

What criteria do you apply for making decisions?

Why did you decide on one particular course of action rather than another?

How much time were you allotted for certain decisions?

In groups of **three**, each principal reports on his prioritization, decisions and reasons and listens to the others, noting similarities and differences. Time is allowed for further discussion and exchange of opinions among the three.

In the full group, participants are asked for their reactions to the INBOX activity, which always arouses thoughtful comments. They note how much they gain from hearing each other's reasons for prioritizing and deciding on a course of action. Many principals comment on how the reflection sparked by the exercise helped them to understand their own motives for making decisions.

The Principals' Center in Times of Crisis: The Murder of Prime Minister Yitzchak Rabin

Written by Ora Zohar on November 6,1995

It is less than 48 hours since all of us here in Israel were electrified by the assassination of Prime Minister Yitzchak Rabin on Saturday night. I want to record my own sense of disorientation and the events of yesterday, Sunday (a school day in Israel), surrounding the planned meeting of the Principals' Center.

At 7:00 AM, I began conversations with other members of the Center staff to consider the possibility of cancelling the three-day session. We were ambivalent for many reasons. Firstly, the Center had been established with a number of goals in mind. A central goal had been to provide a forum for thoughtful discussions for principals. Yesterday, it seemed possible that principals might welcome the opportunity to share their feelings and concerns with their peers; that they might consider what educators in this tragic situation can do to learn and teach lessons crucial to our society's future.

On the other hand, it was also clear that school leaders should be with their school families at this time of heavy mourning. In our telephone calls to the principals, we heard mixed messages. "How can you even think of meeting at a time like this?!" one principal screamed into the phone. Another told us, "I was in school today and I have thoroughly organized tomorrow's program for the school. I want to come, but I don't want to be the only one."

So it went for several hours. We tried to get a clear directive from the Ministry, but none was forthcoming. Principals, we were told, must ensure that their school had an educational program organized for Monday, the day of the funeral, but did not have to be present in school.

As time passed, it became clear that some participants were already on their way to Jerusalem. Of the 40 registered principals, eight had reported they would not attend; ten had called in for clarification; but we had not heard from the others. We were unsure how to understand this silence; did it mean they were coming or were they simply assuming the meeting had been cancelled?

By the time the Hebrew University announced that there would be no classes on Monday, it was already 2:00 P.M., less than two hours before our official opening time. Two of our staff members took over the telephones and tried to reach anyone who might not have set out. We then sat down to plan a session for anyone who might turn up. We asked ourselves the classic questions one asks before any session, but with a greater sense of stress. What could we do that would be valuable to the group?

This was our plan for that day.

1. Hello! Apologize for the mixed messages about this meeting. Explain both our thinking and the confusion of the University. Note present plan to be together for two hours, have dinner and disperse.

2. Ask each person to introduce himself and his school.

3. Ask each person to describe what happened at their school on Sunday.

4. Consider or hear what they had planned for the school program on Monday.

5. Remind us all that there are stages of mourning, from *shiva* (seven days) to *shloshim* (thirty days), to the year, requiring different behavior for each stage. Suggest that we begin to think of how we might plan for each stage in our own school. What educational issues do we want to emphasize? The basic moral issue of violence and murder? The social implications of hatred within a society? Responding to anxieties and fears of the children? Constructive ways of expressing grief and loss? For each of these issues, how can we reach the pupils, staff, and parents?

6. Work in small groups, with individuals first writing the educational issues most relevant or pressing in their own context. Then each group clarifies the issues and brainstorms strategies and activities.

7. We decided to distribute copies of Yitzhak Rabin's famous speech of 1967 on the Hebrew University Campus when he received an Honorary Doctorate. We thought it was useful to have a text that each principal could choose to use at any stage during the coming month.

This was our planned MENU and now this is what actually happened. Thirteen principals showed up and their reports about the events of Sunday were impressive and heartwarming. One principal broke down while describing the special events her pupils had arranged. Others quietly took notes. There was a strong sense of sharing and of learning.

Some of the principals had arrived angry because we had not managed to reach them. Nevertheless, several hours later, when the group broke up, everyone expressed the feeling that the hours spent together were helpful and rewarding. They felt they were given specific ideas and strategies for meeting the short and long-range challenges that lay ahead. They were taking home renewed strength and confidence to face the difficulties of those black days.

What did we, the Staff, learn from the tension, indecision and stress of the experience? We relearned two basic truths; that it is not always easy to be sure of what to do, and that the conception of the Principals' Center as a resource for principals is valid in times of crisis as well as normal times.

What Principals Had to Say about their Experience

Beginning in 2005 a core group of 16 graduates of the Principals' Center participated in a study intended as a first step towards writing the current book. They responded generously in a preliminary questionnaire, in in-depth interviews, and in a focus group. The study explored their thoughts and reflections on a number of key aspects of their experience as principals.

Below are some of the participants' overall memories of the Center experience and atmosphere:

Getting to Know Other Prinicipals

- *Respect was the key. We found in the Center people who believed that principals' work is of value, and related to us accordingly.*

- *Meeting other principals in the Center gave us a sense of togetherness, helped to fight the general isolation of the role. I saw that I was not alone with my problems, and I learned from the others and how they related to similar issues.*

- *Even when there were disagreements, they were about issues, and in a safe atmosphere of mutual respect.*

- *It was interesting to meet principals from different sectors. Suddenly you heard an angle you never thought of before and are amazed to hear.*

- *We learned to attend, to listen to each other. Attending is crucial for principals and for teachers. So many people need attention!*

Relating to Staff

- *I became more aware of the centrality of teachers in schools, and of the importance of my nurturing them so that they could in turn nurture their students.*

- *I realized the importance of including teachers more actively in decision-making and giving public recognition to outstanding teachers.... I understood that I may have the vision, but in the final analysis I can only implement it if teachers, in partnership, make it happen.*

- *I learned from the Center to sit down with every teacher after I observe a class. In our discussion, I always start with something positive, and then ask for his own reflections on the lesson.*

An Experience of Connectedness

- *After each session I returned home with new spirit, new strength, different ways of looking at things, and more empathy in general. I was more aware of the need for Connectedness, of the role of adults in school life, of pupils' needs, of my own role to nurture teachers.*

- *The human angle took on a larger role — the centrality of Connectedness, of bonding, of empathy.*

- *I learned that above and beyond the academic learning the inclusive, supportive, respectful, empowering atmosphere was essential for effective learning.*

In a subsequent meeting held at the University between Center Staff members and graduates of the Principals' Center who over the years had been promoted to senior positions in the Ministry of Education, former principals were asked to answer in writing, "What did you take from the Principals' Center that helped you in your new role at the

Ministry?" We have gleaned the following from their written responses and the ensuing lively and joyful discussion (not conclusive and not in any order of importance):

- the skill of leading a staff;
- the awareness to be sensitive to the personal needs of staff members;
- to be aware of the needs of the "other";
- a box of relevant tools for my new position;
- the necessity and benefits of writing and documentation of events;
- the ability to handle conflicts skillfully;
- the awareness that I am responsible and accountable;
- the strength to withstand and not to surrender to bureaucracy;
- the ability to see things from different perspectives;
- the obligation to present challenges to all workers;
- the importance of creating a happy and nurturing work environment;
- not to be satisfied with the status quo; to constantly create anew and innovate;
- the importance of an independent and responsible staff.

Letters to a New Principal

We will conclude this chapter with three Letters to a New Principal written by principals, graduates of our Center, who participated in the study described earlier.

Dear New Principal,

Hello! You have just now gotten word that you have been chosen for the job you have so wanted for so long – school principal! I am sure that for days and nights you have been thinking about this moment; you've made plans, you've checked, asked questions, made clarifications, and now you feel you know exactly what you are going to do!

Just before you embark on your new role in life, I would like to share a few words with you, words from the heart, words from thirteen years on the job.

As a school principal you have many resources. But remember, the most important resource, far greater than any other, is the human resource, your human capital. I am referring to the school's teachers and workers, the pupils and their parents, and all of the outside agents such as the supervisors and the municipal education workers.

Before you charge ahead, think about all of the people who surround you in your new position: The vice principal and the senior management staff, your secretary, the maintenance man, and the cleaning staff. In your first staff meeting, present your visions and goals and expectations of the members of the staff. Learn to listen to them and pay careful attention to what they say. Be open and forthright and find out where their ambitions and visions meet your ambitions and visions. Find out what motivates them and be sensitive to their needs. Share your thoughts and perspectives with them. On this common ground, build bridges for constructive exchange of ideas. These people will then become involved in your plans and visions for the school, not following orders out of fear but out of a sense of identification and partnership.

The power of authority is important but do your best not to use it. Its influence is limited and what's more, it can take you places you don't want to go! Don't just give orders. Explain your rationale and your goals. Learn to take constructive criticism as well as give it. If something you requested was not done, always ask why. You will find that often it was due to some unavoidable difficulty, ignorance, or fear and not to laziness, disrespect or impudence. If you show willingness to be of help in completing the task, you will find that you have made a loyal partner for the future.

On the personal side, each one of your workers is a whole person with a full life outside of the school walls, a life of desires, needs, satisfactions and difficulties. These people want you to "see" them, to know and understand them. Take interest in what is going on in their personal lives. Try to remember what little gestures that your previous boss did that made you feel good and avoid the ones that caused you hard feelings.

Be flexible enough to admit mistakes but stand by your principles. Consistency is crucial to your success. People in your school need to know they can count on you to be clear and transparent in all that you do.

Wishing you great success….
Vered Marom, Rishon Lezion

$$\smile \quad \smile \quad \smile$$

To the New Partner in Mission,

I have deliberated a great deal before actually sitting down to write this letter. On the one hand, you deserve my congratulations and esteem for having survived the whole hiring process, and for joining this most important group in whose hands the most precious of all are entrusted. On the other hand, you have entered a system in which you will be addicted to work day and night, in which you won't forgive yourself if you have a single minute in which you are sitting and doing nothing and not thinking about your mission.

The responsibility is weighty, expectations high as the sky. The system of interests and resources that distributes powers and pushes in different and often contradictory directions is complex and confusing.

I asked a group of teachers in our school for their input on how to advise you. I would like to share with you the results of this brief discussion:

- *A new principal needs to ask God for the Wisdom of Solomon, so that he acts with integrity and wisdom.*

- *Give every teacher and worker a number of opportunities accompanied by guidance and consulting before judging his abilities. Do not judge teachers or workers at first sight or in a first meeting. Never judge people on the basis of rumors and gossip.*

- *Create a positive environment of support, teamwork, morale, and mutual learning among staff members, and be both leader and partner in this process.*

- *Open your door to listen to and give guidance to teachers, parents, and pupils. Act with love and assertiveness, both important pillars to school management.*

- *Continually evaluate the school's teaching and evaluation process. The principal's main job is to be concerned about and to lead to a better future for the pupils.*

- *Have teachers participate in decision making to the extent possible in areas related to their work. The more the teacher is a partner to the decision, the more the decision is likely to be implemented out of an inner motivation rather than as obedience to authority.*

- *Have parents and pupils participate in setting the school's strategy, and in making other decisions that require their involvement.*

- *Be the head of the family, the father and the mother of the family of teachers and workers. Listen, support, share, contain, guide, direct, consult, empower and be open to different and varied opinions.*

In addition to these important points from the discussion with the teachers, I wanted to add two more categories.

Don'ts!

- *Don't erase the past. Appreciate what was, at the same time that you look at what needs to be. Build a new bridge from the past to a promising future. Plan or update, together with the staff, the school strategy (mission, vision, values, school convention, goals, smart objectives and activities) and move forward in implementation through the planning of activities.*

- *Don't spread yourself thin. Don't invest your energies and those of your staff in many initiatives and projects. Focus on two, no more than three initiatives each year.*

- *Don't become addicted to work. Plan quality leisure time for you and your family. This will enable you to stay fresh; and in this way you will be able to be more effective in your mission.*

Be an Example!

- *Be an example in speech and in action. Your words, what you say about the vision, the mission, the slogans, the objectives and values will speak and look better through your actions.*

- *Be an example and keep learning. It is very important that you take part in training programs designated for principals in the areas that are helpful to a new principal. Each year choose at least one serious program that interests you. The program is not just the material presented, it is much beyond approach and style, it is especially an opportunity for mutual learning among peers. Learn, think, share and choose the one that best fits and will most contribute to your school. Implement the ideas together with the staff.*

- *Be an example in listening to teachers, to pupils and parents. Hear their comments, their suggestions and their opinions, and do what is best for the school.*

- *Be an example in initiative, be an entrepreneur. Each year choose two issues and focus on them. Lead the process but invite others to be your partners and give them the authority. At least one of the plans will succeed.*

- *Be an example in your professionalism. Make decisions based on the professional gathering and analysis of data. Learn and analyze the achievements of the pupils on both the internal and external tests and tasks.*

Welcome to this most important job, in which our society's sons and daughters are handed to you, in which you are enabled to lead these people, little in body but great in soul and spirit, to a bigger and better future.

Congratulations and have a successful journey.
Aziz Da'im, Haifa

🍎 🍎 🍎

Dear New Principal,

Being a principal of a high school is a very complex, difficult and challenging task. It demands an unceasing effort of checking and analyzing every planned activity in relation to how goals are set, how objectives are executed, and how they are evaluated, while paying a great deal of attention to feedback.

You, the principal, must always remember that day in and day out, every hour of every day, your leadership is being tested - by your teachers, your pupils, your parents, the Ministry of Education, your supervisors, and even the local media. But your greatest degree of commitment and accessibility is to your teachers and pupils.

From my experience, I offer you a number of points to consider:

- *Proclaim school policy with regard to rules of conduct and discipline. Emphasize the importance of an Open Door policy – be accessible to every pupil, teacher and parent. This policy invites others to enter, to be seen, to ask for help, and to comment. The principal's door is physically open and there is no need to go through a secretary. The same procedure should be implemented by senior staff.*

- *Don't be a soloist – talk issues over as much as possible with your teachers and pupils before making decisions. How? Personal conversations and joint meetings.*

- *Strive to create a safe and nurturing environment, whether in terms of maintenance of the building and yard, or in terms of creating agreed upon behavioral norms for teachers and pupils.*

- *Show presence – Walk around the school several times every day while greeting every pupil and teacher. The purpose of wandering around is to make an ongoing check of the maintenance of the school, its aesthetics and the relative quiet in the halls during class time. Pass on your comments and instructions following this patrol to the appropriate functionaries.*

- *Management meetings – at least once a week (for two hours). Plan the content of the meetings carefully. This is where the decisions that will have the greatest impact on school life and* climate should be made. Each position-holder updates the group on successes and problems, the information is then examined and evaluated, and decisions are made. As principal, you must behave as first among equals, to listen and in the end to express an opinion. In the final analysis, the decision is a joint one.

- *Staff lounge* – spend time in the staff lounge during the break. Be with your teachers and join them in small talk. You are one of them.

- *Nurture your teachers and your entire staff. Give each one attention. Initiate meetings with them and get to know each one of them. These personal conversations are important in order to enable people to feel at ease and open, leading to feelings of togetherness, caring and family.*

- *Student government* – as principal you should nurture the student government and participate in some of its meetings. It is an important tool for getting feedback about satisfaction. Appoint a creative teacher to lead and provide guidance to the student leaders, who are themselves an important tool for influencing the student body and for organizing social and cultural activities.

- *Strive for excellence, in exemplary behavior, in fair play, in mutual aid, mutual respect, and generosity.*

- *Encourage varied initiatives in all areas.*

- *Remember: Leadership is measured in doing, in standing up to pressures, in the willingness to take responsibility, in the desire to bring benefit to others, and in success.*

And the rest, go now and learn!

Sincerely,
Yoel Ortal, Kfar Saba

Chapter 8
The Mechanech Program and Mt. Scopus College, Melbourne, Australia

Introduction

In 1980, Mt. Scopus College (a Jewish high school in Melbourne, Australia) established a consultative relationship with the Melton Center of the Hebrew University in Jerusalem. The Melton Center hoped to introduce an innovative program of Jewish values into the curriculum, and had been working with members of the Jewish Studies faculty to that end. It seemed to the Melton staff that it would be helpful if a general climate of change could be developed, as a readiness-for-change would facilitate the entry of any innovation. In addition, there was a feeling among general (non-Jewish) studies faculty that the school was investing disproportionally in the professional development of the Jewish Studies sector.

Knowing that the National Center for Staff Development of Hebrew University had worked for a number of years with multi-disciplinary school staffs in Israel, England and South Africa developing professional awareness, skills and collegiality, the Melton Center invited the National Center to lead workshops for the teachers of Mount Scopus College.

The goals of these workshops were 1) to create a climate of readiness for change; 2) to create a sense of professional collegiality; and 3) to provide structured opportunities for professional dialogue among teachers of all grade levels, departments and campuses of Mount Scopus College.

This was the beginning of what was to become the *Mechanech* Program to develop the role of pastoral care in a school. The intervention took place between October 1983 and February 1990. To this day, Mount Scopus college continues to implement the model.

Goals of First Visit

In July, 1981, Chava Greenberg and Dr. Ora Zohar spent two weeks in the Mount Scopus College community. In addition to directing workshops with 44 teachers from K-12, they met with pupils, parents and alumni in order to learn more about the school.

Chava and Ora were surprised and impressed by the strength of a single message transmitted to them by all members of the Scopus world with whom they met. This was the message of emotional alienation from the school, of a sense of de-personalization, of the unimportance of the individual – whether pupil or teacher – in the existing value system of the school. Involvement in the school was very task-oriented and the underlying goal was: "Get our children into university!"

Identifying a Problem

Chava and Ora documented this message of emotional alienation in a de-personalized environment in their initial report to the Board of Governors of Mt. Scopus College. Despite the existing organizational structure of conveners, counselors, and senior masters and mistresses, an overwhelming number of teachers and pupils reported a virtual lack of non-academic related interactions between school adults and schoolchildren. The school's size (2700 pupils) was a source of great pride to the Melbourne Jewish community in general, and to the Board of Governors in particular – but that very size seemed to be counter-productive to the personalization of the school.

A Possible Solution

The report suggested that Mount Scopus College could develop a more personal, less alienating climate without detracting from academic excellence. The Israeli *Mechanech* model – pastoral care for each class (rather than per level) was presented as an example of an organizational program providing built-in personalization for both students and staff. A *mechanech* is not a glorified clerk and keeper of records; he is an educator in the fullest sense of the word. He is a guide for his pupils' journey through adolescence, a journey into responsible adulthood. The challenge is to make that journey as warm, companionable, and safe as possible for our children.

The Mission

Following the initial report, the Board of Governors invited the Center to conceptualize, introduce and develop an appropriate model of pastoral care for Mt. Scopus College. That invitation was to lead to a decade of intense involvement in the school by the Center with seven subsequent visits by Center staff to Melbourne and six seminars for Scopus College staff in Jerusalem.

The *Mechanech* Program

The Center believed that the introduction of *Mechanchim* to Scopus would lead to a significant difference in the real and perceived climate of the school. This belief launched the intervention that came to be known as The *Mechanech* Program.

The goals of the program were as follows:

1. To designate one teacher per class (the *Mechanech*) with clear responsibilities for providing pastoral care to each child in the class.

2. To create a class climate of support and acceptance, encouraging pupils' sense of belonging to a home group.

3. To provide parents with a specific caring adult to consult with about their child's personal, social, and academic development.

4. To provide teachers with a professional role which would encourage significant involvement with pupils, both individually and as a cohesive group.

The Intervention Process

The intervention process began in October 1983 with on-site training of 14 teachers who were to pioneer the role. That group spent two and one-half weeks of further training in Jerusalem in December '83/January '84 and, in February, 1984. At the start of the school year, all seventh- and eighth-grade classes opened with *Mechs* (the nickname for *Mechanchim*) in place.

From 1983 to 1988, pre-service training of new *Mechs*, and in-service training for veteran *Mechs* took place both in Melbourne and in Jerusalem. During those years, the *Mech* role, begun in seventh and eighth grades, spread, as originally planned, upwards to the ninth through twelfth grades. The program was perceived as meeting a real need in upper primary grades as well, and *Mechanchim* for fifth and sixth grades were trained during 1987-88.

The Evaluation

The Board of Governors had invested funds both in training *Mechanchim* in Melbourne and in Jerusalem and in an enlarged payroll due to the extra hours put in by *Mechanchim*. Furthermore, professional literature on educational innovation is rich in descriptions of intervention programs introduced by outside consultants that began with a burst of enthusiasm and high hopes but disappeared soon after they left the scene. Thus in 1989, five years after the program's introduction into the school, both the Board of Governors and the change agents in Jerusalem agreed on the importance of evaluating the intervention with an emphasis on its impact as perceived by participants.

Researchers of change note that change is always difficult but that there is a hierarchy of difficulty. It is easiest to change knowledge, harder to change attitudes and hardest to change behavior. An evaluation of the *Mechanech* program, thus, sought answers to the following questions:

1. Could the model of pastoral care be transplanted successfully from Jerusalem to Melbourne?

2. Could it take root and remain entrenched after the change agents left?

3. Would changes in behavior appear in the interpersonal relations between pupils and *Mechanchim*, and parents and *Mechanchim*?

4. Finally, would the climate of Mt. Scopus College then be perceived as being more personal and warm?

In February 1990, exactly 6 years after the first *Mechanchim* initiated their new roles, Chava and Ora made their fourth and sixth trip, respectively, to conduct the field work for the evaluation study. The evaluation included four distinct yet complementary parts:

1. A survey of pupils designed to measure their level of utilization of the program and their level of satisfaction with it. The survey was administered to about 1000 pupils from grades 7 to 12;

2. A survey of parents designed to measure their level of awareness and utilization of the program and their level of satisfaction with it. 585 parents participated in the survey, consisting of a specially-designed questionnaire administered to parents of pupils from grades 7 to 12;

3. In-depth interviews with 42 parents;

4. A series of individual and group discussions with *Mechanchim*.

In the evaluations, the following questions were asked:

- Did pupils perceive the *Mechanech* as a resource person available to them?

- Did they utilize the *Mechanech* for help in academic difficulties? in social difficulties? in personal difficulties?

- Did parents perceive their child's *Mechanech* as a resource person available to them?

- Did parents turn to the *Mechanech* when their child had academic difficulties? when their child had personal difficulties with other teachers? when their child had social problems?

- Overall, did pupils and parents consider the new role of *Mechanech* important/essential to the quality of school life at Mt. Scopus College?

- Did *Mechanchim* themselves perceive their role as having made Mt. Scopus College a more personal school, and their relations with pupils more satisfying and rewarding?

Findings

General

Analyses of the information obtained from all four sectors of data collection revealed an overwhelming support and enthusiasm for the *Mechanech* Program. More than three-quarters of all pupils and over 90% (!) of parents thought the *Mechanech* Program was important or even essential for the school.

Pupils' Survey

It is clear that the ultimate clients of any school are the pupils. Pupils spend many thousands of hours in school in the formative years of their lives. Too many adults have told bitterly of their unhappy school experiences. Too many pupils in schools today confirm that those memories are as valid as ever. In the original Greenberg- Zohar visit, Mt. Scopus pupils had complained of a sense of depersonalization and alienation. Many pupils and alumni told Greenberg and Zohar that teachers cared only about grades, homework, and getting pupils into the universities so that the school would keep a good name. Great efforts had gone into educating Scopus subject-centered teachers into their new pastoral role. Availability to pupils was a central element of that role. Thus a key question in the evaluation was whether that message had been effectively delivered to the pupil-consumer. It was important to find out if pupils realized that their *Mechanchim* were available to them.

More than three quarters of pupils perceived their *Mechanech* as available to them at any time at school or at home. Twenty percent perceived their *Mechanech* as available at specific times and four percent perceived their *Mechanech* as rarely or never available.

Use Pupils Made of the Mechanech Program

We noted that it is easier to change knowledge and attitudes than it is to change behavior. We wanted to know if pupils made use of the availability of their *Mechanchim*, and if so, in what instances. Were pupil-teacher interactions still limited to academic issues, or would pupils now turn to the *Mechanech* for personal and social concerns?

Table 1 demonstrates that seventy percent of Scopus pupils would turn to *Mechanchim* about social problems with peers, and sixty-two percent would turn to *Mechanchim* about personal problems with other teachers. It is interesting to note that pupils made a clear distinction between these concerns and academic difficulties. Only thirty percent would turn first to the *Mechanech* on subject problems, with sixty percent going first to the subject teacher. Figure 1 is strong evidence that Scopus pupils understood the role of the *Mechanech* and behaved accordingly.

Table 1: The Use Pupils Made of the *Mechanech* Program

ASPECT	ITEM	AGREE
Social	If I were unhappy socially in my class, I would talk to my *Mech.*	70%
Pupil-Teacher Relations	If I had troubles getting on with a subject teacher, I would first talk with my *Mech.*	62%
Academic	If I had a problem with my studies, I would talk to my *Mech.* my subject teacher.	30% 60%

Parents' Survey

Pupils are a school's ultimate client, but parents are crucial partners in the educational endeavor of any school. In private schools, moreover, parents make the basic decision of whether to enroll or withdraw their child from a school. The strengthening of home-school ties and the broadening of those ties from academic to personal-social issues was a clear goal of the *Mechanech* Program.

We wanted to see if parents perceived that *Mechanchim* were available to them and if they would turn to *Mechanchim* with non-academic concerns.

Three-quarters of the parents perceived that *Mechanchim* were available at any time at school or at home. Less happily, almost one-fifth of the parents felt that the *Mechanchim* were rarely or never available.

Use Parents Made of the Mechanech Program

Perhaps of even greater interest than parents' perception of *Mechanchim* availability is their view of the *Mechanech* as a resource person for help concerning their children.

- Eighty-seven percent of parents reported they would turn to their child's *Mechanech* about a child's social problems in class.

- Eighty percent would turn to the *Mechanech* if another teacher complained about their child's behavior.

- More than three quarters would turn to the *Mechanech* for information about academic progress.

As for parents' expectations of the *Mechanech*, a whopping ninety percent would expect the *Mechanech* to turn to them if the child seemed unhappy, or had social problems with classmates, as shown in Table 2.

Table 2: The Use Parents Made of the *Mechanech* Program

ASPECT	ITEM	RESPONSE
Social	I WOULD turn to my child's *Mechanech* for help if:	Agree
	My child had social problems in class.	87%
	Other teachers complained about my child's behavior.	80%
	I WOULD NOT expect my child's *Mechanech* to turn to me if:	Disagree
	My child had social problems in class.	89%
	My child seemed unhappy over a period of time.	92%
Academic	I WOULD turn to my child's *Mechanech*:	Agree
	For information about his academic performance.	76%
	If other teachers were dissatisfied with my child's academic progress.	62%

ASPECT	ITEM	RESPONSE
Academic	I WOULD NOT expect my child's *Mechanech* to turn to me:	Disagree
	If other teachers were dissatisfied with my child's academic progress.	83%

Impact of the Mechanech's Role on Personalization of Mount Scopus School

The results thus far indicated that *Mechanchim* were perceived as essential or important, as being highly available and as the school person to turn to for personal and/or social concerns by both pupils and parents. Did this make a difference in the climate of Mt. Scopus College? Did the personalization of the *Mechanech*-pupil and *Mechanech*-parent relationships contribute to the overall atmosphere of the school, which they had criticized in 1982?

Eighty percent of parents expressed their sense that the *Mech* role helped make Mt. Scopus school a warm and friendly school.

In-Depth Interviews with Parents

In February 1990, Chava Zohar and Dr. Ora Zohar interviewed 42 parents of pupils at Mt. Scopus College. Each interview lasted one to one and a half hours. A review of these conversations gave clear evidence of the following:

1. The parents knew that their child had a *Mech*.

2. Overall, they were satisfied with their *Mech*'s performance.

3. There were parents who had had extremely negative experiences with their child's *Mech* and were quite bitter, complaining of indifference or laziness or both.

4. There were parents who had had extraordinarily positive *Mech* experiences and they sang the praises of concerned devoted *Mechanchim* who had given of their time and efforts far beyond the expected norms.

It was this element of the evaluation that highlighted a truth that we all knew intuitively: The *Mechanech* Program was as strong, or as weak, as the individual human being in the role. For pupils and for their parents, the person in the role made the critical difference. The school can assign role power but in the final analysis, it is personal power that brings significance to the inter-personal relationships of all those involved. Case studies as reported by parents ranged from casual callousness to empathic generosity of concern and of self.

Discussions with Mechanchim

Throughout the years, Center staff had maintained an ongoing if informal correspondence with friends on the Scopus staff. We had a particularly strong relationship with Barbara Black, the chairperson of the *Mechanech* Department. Our 1990 meetings with both veteran and newer *Mechanchim* confirmed what we had been hearing.

There were two prevalent perceptions *Mechanchim* had about their new role in the school:

1. The role was difficult, time-consuming and often intrusive in personal or family time.

2. The psychic rewards were great.

Another facet of the *Mechanech* role is the responsibility for productive weekly class meetings. Many *Mechanchim* found these class meetings a challenge to their creativity. Others found them taxing and often non-productive.

The *Mechanech* found himself caught in a delicate web which is the nature of the role itself; it brings with it both burden and reward. *Mechanchim* often carry pupils' pain, anger, or failure home with them as surely as they take home notebooks or examinations to mark, and this kind of take-home work exacts an emotional toll. The flip side of the coin, of course, is that the satisfactions of genuine relationships with youngsters are deeply rewarding. For many teachers, this is what drew them into the profession in the first place.

Summary

The findings of this evaluation can be summarized as follows:

1. The transplant of the Israel model of the *Mechanech* to Australia was successful. The intervention became an

accepted, taken-for-granted part of Mt. Scopus College life, from fifth to twelfth grades.

2.   Overwhelmingly, Mt. Scopus College pupils and their parents appreciated the *Mechanech*, saw him as available and turned to him with academic, personal and social concerns.

3.   Parent expectations of the *Mechanech* were very high and usually met. When individual *Mechanchim* did not meet them, parents felt cheated and angry.

4.   *Mechanchim* enjoyed the role, but found it very demanding.

Suggestions for Strengthening the *Mechanech* Program

Results of the evaluation provided gratifying evidence that the systematic introduction into a school of a new teaching role – the *Mechanech* or pastoral care teacher – could lead to significant and positive involvement of the adults in a school community in the lives of children and youth. This finding demonstrates that significance in education requires not only teachers with interpersonal and pedagogical skills, but also school structures and culture that make significance a priority. Two specific recommendations were made to the school that reflect this insight:

1.   All teachers are potentially significant in the lives of their pupils, but *Mechanchim* are in a position to be especially so. It is vital that teachers high in interpersonal skills and with strong interest in pupils be actively sought out to take on *Mechanech* responsibilities. School administration often must choose between assigning subject hours or *Mech* hours to a particular teacher. How that choice is made reflects the priorities of the administration.

2.   An area of the *Mechanech* Program that indicates the need for further thought is the weekly hour designed for class meetings. This hour is meant to provide prime time for group building activities, for *Mech*-class dialogue, for many kinds of informal education, for guest speakers and for special events or problems that arise. Evaluation data suggested that further effort should be invested in strengthening these hours.

Echoes from the Mechanech Program in Toronto

The positive response from pupils, parents and staff at Mt. Scopus encouraged us to accept an invitation to duplicate the Mechanech program at a school ten thousand miles away – the Bialik School in Toronto, Canada. A different school, a different school culture…. not Israel, not Australia. Bialik is a jewel of a school, smaller, cozier, a Kindergarten to eighth grade school.

Could the same program flourish again, in another transplant? Our belief in the role and the pleasure at their response led us to agree to try.

We went to Toronto…. We met new wonderful friends…. They requested the training…. And here are some echoes from their experience:

🍎 🍎 🍎

When I walked into the room at the Board of Jewish Education in Toronto on that important winter day in 1994, I did not know what to expect from the ladies from Israel who were going to talk to us about being Mechanchim. I barely knew what that word meant, let alone what would be expected of me. I began to understand what you meant by connectedness. You opened up a whole new world for me and you have been my role models ever since. The seminar has put a permanent stamp on who I am as an educator and for that I am eternally grateful.

🍎 🍎 🍎

Following the wonderful words of wisdom and encouragement that you shared at our last sessions, we are delighted that Mechanech meeting times are now reality and part of the new contract. Your impressing on the group the importance of regular group meetings clearly carried weight.

🍎 🍎 🍎

I can't believe the years have flown by so quickly since our training in Israel and Toronto. The seminar you directed had such an impact on my personal and professional life. As a Mechanechet, I felt I was able to be more than just a teacher. I grew to understand students differently and felt I had more impact on their lives by applying techniques and strategies you gave us. I will never forget our days together and the true love and devotion you showed to all of us.

...In my capacity as Vice Principal, I continue to use all that I learned in our seminar. I am currently teaching our fourth graders to be Recess Buddies and our fifth graders to be Peacemakers, so each lesson I begin with HIGHLIGHTS and Since We Last Met... It always amazes me what information those activities yield. Our time spent together was a phenomenal learning experience and one which has served me well both in my personal and professional capacity...I thank you from the bottom of my heart.

Ora's students in front of "our darling little hut", 1967

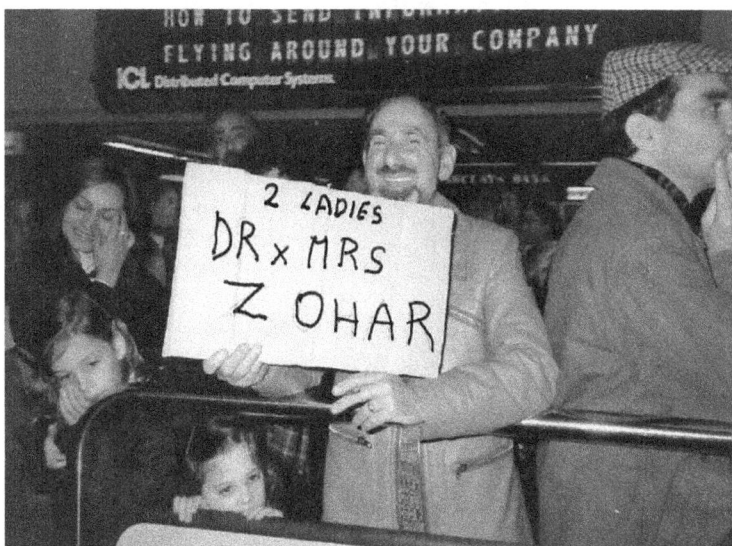

Dr. Ora Zohar and Mrs. Chava Zohar arrive at Heathrow Airport for their first
international workshop in 1982

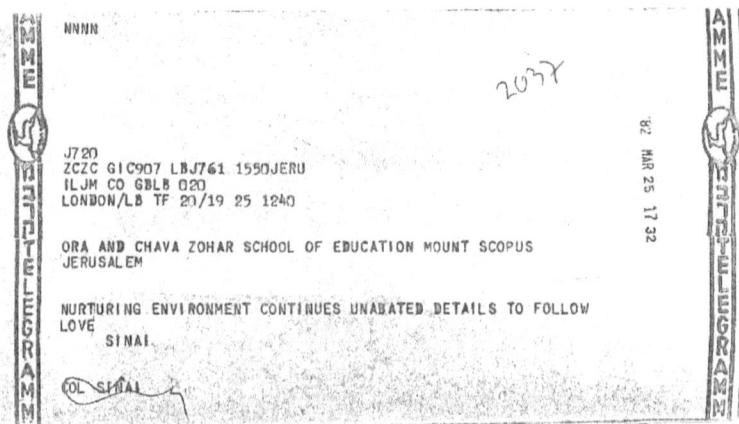

```
NNNN

J7 20
ZCZC GIC907 LBJ761 1550JERU
ILJM CO GBLB 020
LONDON/LB TF 20/19 25 1240

ORA AND CHAVA ZOHAR SCHOOL OF EDUCATION MOUNT SCOPUS
JERUSALEM

NURTURING ENVIRONMENT CONTINUES UNABATED DETAILS TO FOLLOW
LOVE
      SINAI

COL SINAI
```

Echoes from our work with the Sinai School, London, 1982

First graduating class of elementary school principals at the Principals' Center, 1986

Principals at work in a workshop in Bournemouth, England, 1985

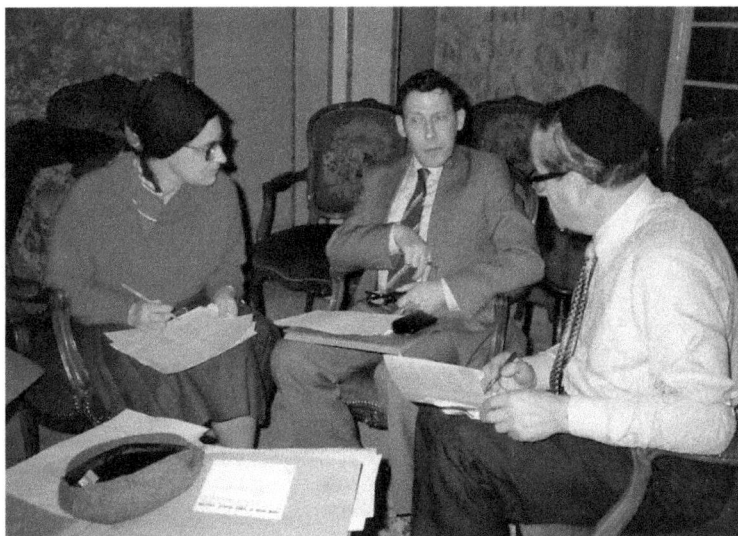

Teachers at work in a small group in the Bialik School in Toronto

Chava Greenberg at work with school staff in Beit Jan, a Druze village in northern Israel

Staff from a Druze school in Usafia, meeting in the Jerusalem home of Chava Zohar

Ora Zohar (l) and Rachel Karni (r) with staff members of the Mount Scopus School in Melbourne, Australia

Eighth graduating class of the Principals' Center, high school principals, at Hebrew University Mount Scopus campus, overlooking the old city of Jerusalem, 1996

The RICH staff, from left: Aviva Pinchuk, Arleen Eidelman, and Susan Haber

Chapter 9
RICH – A Curriculum for Significance

Introduction[9]

RICH (Relevant Issues in Contemporary Humanism) is a curriculum designed for English language study in the upper high school grades which confronts pupils with value issues. Created by Dr Ora Zohar with Arleen Edelman, Susan Haber, and Aviva Pinchuk, the program reflects the Center's democratic, humanistic approach to the content of teaching.

In the context of Victor Frankl's book, *Man's Search for Meaning,* Ora explains, "Meaningfulness is one of the basic needs of life. The teacher becomes more significant if she/he is dealing with issues that are important to the pupils. She should share and discuss values with the pupils. There is little of this in the schools and teachers are given little direction in value education.

"Since so many hours a week are devoted to the study of English, we suggest that the time can also be used for clarifying values, initiating a quest for meaning. The English program must, of course, help the pupil achieve a certain competence in reading writing and speaking. Why not use the many hours devoted to English to read about and discuss values? As educators, we must go beyond syntax, beyond structure to the deepest issues of life!"

The RICH book consists of a series of themes such as Homelessness and Refugees, Family, Love and Friendship, Decision Making, and Old Age. It is a compilation of prose, fiction, and poetry. Most of the material comes from English literature and journalism, but there are also translations from other languages including Hebrew.

---

[9] Based on an article by Rochelle Furstenberg which appeared in THE JERUSALEM POST on August 30, 1985.

The RICH staff decided to compile a unit on Old Age because in a previous unit on Decision Making, pupils were asked, "What are the decisions a person makes during various stages in his life?" The pupils mentioned decisions made during childhood, decisions concerning marriage, profession, where to live; but when they were asked about Old Age, they felt that old people no longer made decisions. The way they spoke out about the elderly convinced the staff that they must write a unit on Old Age.

After a lesson which included Avraham's Shlonsky's poem, *Three Old Women,* which depicts children repelled by the touch of old women, the class was asked for their reaction to the unit. One pupil replied, "I don't like it. It's so true. It hurts too much."

This reaction indicated to the RICH staff that the unit succeeds in sensitizing pupils to the subject. But the unit also portrays old people as active, engaging people who have much to contribute as expressed by an ancient Chinese proverb included for discussion; *A family that has an old person in it has a jewel.*

Assignments often involve discussing the issues with peers and family. One mother was pleasantly surprised when her child asked her what she thought of romantic love. "My children never thought I had an opinion on these things," she said.

One of the most important aspects of the RICH program is, perhaps, that it integrates Jewish values into the curriculum in a natural way. The program had its beginnings when Rabbi Dr Daniel Tropper was a consultant to former Minister of Education Zevulun Hammer on deepening Jewish identity and bringing Jewish values into the curriculum. He initiated courses in History and Hebrew Literature which integrate an analysis of Jewish values into the general curriculum. He invited Dr Ora Zohar and her staff to do likewise through the teaching of English. "RICH brings Jewish sources alongside other sources. Why should we quote Confucius and not Maimonides? " asks Ora.

Because of the enthusiasm for the first book of RICH, we were asked to publish a simplified version so that less proficient matriculation pupils could benefit from the material as well. The result, *A RICH CHOICE* was published in 1987 followed by Book Two of RICH– *OTHERS: Portraits of Diversity, Pain, and Promise,* dealing with the issue of Prejudice.

It is interesting to note, that although the RICH books were intended for the teaching of English as a Second Language in Israel, the books were in great demand for study in many schools abroad: in Melbourne, Budapest, Mexico City, Toronto, New York as well as in summer camps!

🍎 🍎 🍎

Below is the introductory letter to the Teacher's Guide of RICH followed by the letter to the Pupil in the Pupil's Book:

Dear Colleague,

In his beautiful book, Man's Search for Meaning, *Victor Frankl describes his experience in concentration camps and the development of his third school of psychology – logotherapy. Frankl, a psychiatrist-scholar-survivor, believes that a sense of meaning in life gives man the courage and strength to live. Every man's journey through life is a quest for that meaning which will be of special significance for him.*

For many of us, families, friends, or aliya (immigration to Israel) have provided meaning in our personal lives. The need for meaning has proven strong in our professional lives as well. It has led to the desire to imbue teaching with significance beyond skills, syntax or structures. It has impelled a quest for classroom activities involving introspection, reflection and exploration of issues with our pupils. Throughout the years, throughout the country, we have met hundreds of colleagues engaged in a similar quest. They have worked diligently, intuitively and often brilliantly, milking The Enemy, Miss Brill, Eli *or* Eveline *[texts mandated in the English curriculum] for every possible drop of meaning. In recognition of our natural need for a dimension of meaning in our lives as teachers, our responsibility to help pupils initiate their own quest for meaning, and the golden opportunities possible in four or five hours of weekly classroom contact, this program was born.*

The concept is of a series of thematic units, presenting texts and classroom activities in which language skills are involved in a search for meaning. Each unit provides structured opportunities for reading, thinking and talking. The homework assignments reflect educational goals of the program, always offering options and often asking for family involvement. The use of Hebrew texts is deliberate, affirming the integral nature of the program, emphasizing the relevance of Jewish sources to contemporary concerns.

Our interest does not lie in any one answer to questions. It lies in clarifying the obligation schools have to help pupils initiate a personal quest for meaning that will strengthen them and encourage them on their journey into adulthood and through life. It lies in helping teachers to provide a classroom atmosphere and ethos that will generate such a quest. The texts chosen and the wide range of teaching techniques suggested are designed to create just such a climate.

Scores of teachers and their pupils have used RICH units during the pilot years of 1981-84. Their written responses have been heartwarming and extremely helpful. Our visits to their classrooms have confirmed our basic belief that the success of any program depends on intelligent, sensitive teaching. We thank the many wonderful teachers and pupils who were our partners in the past and warmly invite all of you to join us in this partnership.

Sincerely,

The RICH STAFF
Dr Ora Zohar
Arleen Eidelman
Susan Haber
Aviva Pinchuk
Jerusalem, January 1985

🍎 🍎 🍎

Dear Pupil,

You are approaching adulthood, growing physically, emotionally and intellectually. There are many issues to think about, decisions to consider, values to clarify, ideas to explore. All too often, class time in school must focus on material to be taught and knowledge to be gained, leaving very little time for personal and group thought.

Many of you spend more hours in English class than in any other class. For years we have thought of how to use these hours in the most significant way possible. RICH is an attempt to do just that. It is a program designed to provide opportunities for reading, writing, speaking and thinking about important issues within the boundaries of the study of English in the last two years of high school.

We thank those hundreds of pupils who responded so warmly to RICH in its pilot years of 1981-1984 and hope that you and your classmates will find the same pleasure and excitement that they reported.

Sincerely,

The RICH STAFF
Dr Ora Zohar
Arleen Eidelman
Susan Haber
Aviva Pinchuk

To illustrate the RICH approach to building a curriculum for significance we will share here the first lesson plans in the Teacher's Guide for two units: *Roads* and *Invisible Lines*.

Unit Three: ROADS

Lesson One:

Personal choices seriously affect the life one leads. Youth, on the verge of adulthood, face multiple choices, paths, and roads leading in different directions. How does one choose? On what basis is a decision made? How important is each choice? In what ways might a choice affect a future stage of life? Important choices should be made within a clear perceptual framework of a hierarchy of personal values.

Otherwise, they may be made impulsively and thoughtlessly, without consideration of consequences or implications.

In Unit Three, texts and activities are designed to encourage introspection, values clarification, peer discussion and classroom-home interaction. The material suggests that:

- The quality of our individual lives is largely in our own hands.
- Choices and decisions affect that quality.
- Choices should reflect a clear values system.
- Moral man perceives his personal relationship and responsibility to the world he lives in.

The unit has five lessons with the following structure:

Lesson One: The inevitability of crossroads and the importance of choice is presented.

Lesson Two: A search for direction is presented.

Lesson Three: Particular choices are described and explained.

Lesson Four: A psychological and philosophical blue-print for decision-making is suggested.

Lesson Five: Roads *Not* Taken are explored.

Our 11th and 12th grade pupils are at a particular crossroads in their lives. As English teachers, we can focus wholly on their success in English studies…or we can *choose* to play a more significant teaching role. Helping them to consider aspects of choice and personal direction reflects our own hierarchy of teaching values.

SET INDUCTION:

The Road Not Taken

Robert Frost

Two roads diverged in a yellow wood,
And sorry I could not travel both
And be one traveler, long I stood
And looked down one as far as I could
To where it bent in the undergrowth;

Then took the other, as just as fair,
And having perhaps the better claim,
Because it was grassy and wanted wear;
Though as for that the passing there
Had worn them really about the same,

And both that morning equally lay
In leaves no step had trodden black.
Oh, I kept the first for another day!
Yet knowing how way leads on to way,
I doubted if I should ever come back.

I shall be telling this with a sigh
Somewhere ages and ages hence:
Two roads diverged in a wood, and I –
I took the one less traveled by,
And that has made all the difference.

1. Teacher reads *The Road Not Taken* aloud. Pupils listen, books closed.

2. Teacher reads the poem a second time. (Pupils follow the text.)

3. Teacher asks class to find the line in the poem that proves each of the following statements:

   a. The speaker tells us about two paths in a forest.

   b. He could not easily decide how to continue his journey.

   c. He tried to see what lay ahead.

   d. He took the less popular path.

   e. He decided to take the other some other time.

   f. He wasn't sure that he would.

   g. It did not seem to matter which path he took.

4. Teacher reminds class that many literary texts throughout history have used the image of Man as Traveler. This leads into a two-part discussion:

   a.   Journey as a symbol of Life (Everyman as Traveler);

   b.   The speaker-traveler of this poem, and his perceptions of his own personal journey.

Note: For the second part of this discussion, the following three points will probably be raised:

- *The forest as an appropriate image for Life*: This may be contrasted, for example, with the rejected choice of a flat plain, or mountain. The variety of trees and shrubs in a forest, the obstruction to long-range vision, the complexity of undergrowth, and possible sense of being lost when a path bends or disappears may all be suggested as supporting the suitability of the image.

- *The clear message of consequences of actions*, in the *"knowing how way leads on to way."* This concept of life as a chain in which each decision may forge a distinct link should be developed. Historic examples may be useful.

- *The sense of the significance of a choice*, as expressed in *"that has made all the difference."* The poet's *sigh* may suggest.... what...regret? disappointment? This point will be helpful when pupils deal with the homework task of considering the possible meanings of the title of the poem.

5. Teacher asks pairs to share a decision each made in which *"way led on to way"* (3-4 minutes).

6. Teacher asks class, "If the wood is the speaker's life, are we given any hint of his stage of life in this poem?" (Pupils may find the *yellow wood* hint of autumn.)

7. The teacher leads into a brief discussion of choice as a life-long phenomenon.

8. Bridge sentence into next activity. For example: "Let's consider this last point for a few minutes."

On the board:

Stages of Life

Infancy   Childhood   Youth   Adulthood   Old Age

a. Please list decisions an individual might make in each of these stages (silent written activity).

b. Pairs compare lists, discuss, interpret.

c. Pairs read the Hebrew verse from an ancient Jewish source (Translation: There is no path without crossroads) and discuss its relevance today.

d. Pairs read the poem to each other, alternating stanzas. **A** reads stanzas one and three, with **B** reading two and four.

9. Closure: Class reads the poem aloud, all **A's** reading their stanzas and **B's** reading theirs.

Homework:

What do you think the significance of the title might be?

And choose **one** of the following:

1. Write a composition called "Roads I May Travel in the Next Ten Years".

2. Write a composition called "The Wood I Live In", noting the season, undergrowth and roads of your present stage of life.

3. Interview a parent, grandparent, aunt, or uncle. Ask them to tell about a path they took in life that *"has made all the difference."* Report in writing.

Note: In this opening lesson pupils have:

- *Listened* to poetry and to each other;

- *Talked* to each other in pairs and in class discussion;

- *Read* the poem at least three times;

- *Written* a list of choices in different stages of life.

They have also *considered*:

- The central concept of Man (themselves) as travelers through life;

- The inevitability of crossroads (choice) on such a journey;

113

- The consequences and possible significance of each choice;

And *shared*:

- Personal past decisions with particular results;

- Personal perceptions of making choices as a life-long activity.

Homework is designed to encourage:

- *Analysis* of the poem – and

- *Introspection* – or

- *Interaction* with an adult family member.

Dialogues begun as school assignments may develop into more meaningful exchanges.

Unit Six: INVISIBLE LINES

Earlier units were devoted to the value of human life, aspects of family life, decision-making and its consequences for the quality of man's life, insights into the role of the elderly in society, and the role of humor in our lives. This unit considers the diversity, ambiguity and vulnerability of human relationships. There are six basic educational goals for the unit:

1. Pupils will recognize the universal human need for closeness, intimacy and connectedness to others.

2. Pupils will note the range of individual responses to the universal need.

3. Pupils will develop an awareness of the complexity and fragility of connectedness.

4. Pupils will consider ways in which relationships may be nurtured or damaged.

5. Pupils will appreciate that Jewish sages searched for ways to develop harmonious interpersonal relations.

6. Pupils will integrate their own life experiences into the study of the texts.

The unit is perceived as a vivid mosaic in which each selection contributes a particular color and shape to the whole. The presentation suggested is designed to provide a structured learning experience involving analysis of texts, sharing of cognitive and affective responses to texts, interpretation, and group discussion of the issues and concerns dealt with.

Everywhere and always teachers are onstage, models of adult interaction with individuals and groups. Our own stance of respect for and sensitivity to others will enhance our pupils' learning of personal skills in this crucial area of human development.

Unit Six opens with William Blake's eighteenth century poem *A Poison Tree*, a masterpiece of apparent simplicity. Blake compels us to recognize the complexity of human relationships and to consider the deep consequences of acts on all actors in a drama.

1. Teacher reminds class of the rules of "Association", in which individuals present an immediate oral or written response to a given word or phrase. Teacher checks their understanding of this by collecting several oral responses to a word such as: winter, beauty, Jerusalem...

2. Teacher asks class to write their personal associative responses to what will be written on the blackboard.

3. Teacher writes **A   Tree** on the blackboard. Pupils write quietly, very briefly. Teacher collects their responses orally and lists these responses on the board. The blackboard may well look like this:

A	Tree
life	shade
beauty	fruit
growing	roots
strong	leaves
of knowledge	

4. Teacher asks class what happens when we change the board by inserting one word.... and inserts

A Poison Tree

Teacher notes, with pupils, the shock produced by the juxtaposition of the discordant notions of Poison and Tree.

5. Teacher bridges into first reading of the poem (books are closed). For example: "Let us listen carefully to a poem with this title and consider how such a title reflects the poet's intention and statement in the poem."

6. Teacher reads the poem aloud:

A Poison Tree

William Blake

I was angry with my friend:
I told my wrath, my wrath did end.
I was angry with my foe:
I told it not, my wrath did grow.

And I water'd it in fears,
Night and morning with my tears;
And I sunned it with smiles,
And with soft deceitful wiles.

And it grew both day and night,
Til it bore an apple bright;
And my foe beheld it shine,
And he knew that it was mine,

And into my garden stole
When the night had veil'd the pole:
In the morning glad I see
My foe outstretch'd beneath the tree.

7. Teacher asks pupils to write whatever they remember from the reading.

8. Teacher asks pupils to share what they wrote with a neighbor.

9. Pupils open books and read the poem to each other, alternating stanzas.

10. Teacher asks pairs to answer two questions about the poem in writing:

    a. What do we know?

    b. What do we **not** know?

11. Teacher circulates as pairs discuss and write, then collects several answers orally, always asking for the textual basis for answers.

12. Teacher writes *"it"* on the blackboard and asks the class:

    a. How many times *"it"* appears in the poem;

    b. To trace the history of *"it"* in the poem (*"it"* was watered, sunned, etc.).

13. Teacher pulls this discussion together noting that: *"it"*, hate/anger, is clearly a growing thing in the poet's mind and perception, and raises the issue of the fruit (consequences) of hate/anger that is nurtured and fed.

14. Teacher asks the class to consider what has happened to both actors in the dramatic action of the poem and to comment on the double damage done by the poison.

15. Teacher bridges into ROLE PLAY. For example: "The poet does not tell us exactly why he was angry, either with his friend or his foe. All of us, at one time or another, have been angry with other people. Think now of one such time, in which you were hurt or angered by someone, or someone you know was hurt or angered."

    a. Think.

    b. Pairs tell each other about the incident.

    c. ROLE PLAY the Hurt and the Hurter, in which the Hurt takes the initiative (*"told my wrath"*).

Optional

    d. Form new pairs. Tell each other about an incident. Re-play with new partner.

    e.   Teacher asks for comments on the experience of re-playing the same situation with a new partner.

Pupils may realize that:

They themselves acted somewhat differently the second time;

Their second partner responded differently from their first partner.

The point of this exercise, that human behavior varies widely even in response to an identical stimulus, is one worth making with pupils.

16. Hebrew verses:

You shall not hate your kinsman in your heart. Reprove your neighbor. (Leviticus 19)

He who hates his friend is as one who sheds blood. (Jewish proverb)

    a.   Teacher asks to have the two verses read aloud.

    b.   Teacher asks pupils to decide, individually, which verse is more appropriate to the poem.

    c.   Teacher asks pupils to share and explain their decision to a neighbor.

    d.   Teacher asks two speakers for each verse to explain their choice to the class.

Homework:

1.   The title of the poem *A Poison Tree* is a vivid symbol of Blake's statement about interpersonal relations. Discuss, referring to the text.

Choose **one**:

2.   Write a dialogue in which a person *"tells his wrath"* to another. The dialogue must clarify the background of the wrath and give both parties a chance to express their feelings.

3.   Write a letter in which the writer begs forgiveness from someone he has hurt in the past.

4.   Tell the story of the poem to members of your family or to friends not learning this material. Discuss the points made in the poem. Write a report of that discussion.

5. Write a poem on a related theme.

6. *In the morning glad I see my foe outstretch'd beneath the tree.*

   This line reflects how the hatred poisoned both the *"foe"* and the speaker. Explain.

Note:

In this opening lesson pupils have seen the powerful consequences of a particular interaction between two people and have considered the implications for all interactions and relationships. They have thought about a painful event known to them, shared this with a peer, and had a chance to rehearse a "telling of wrath." They have been asked to consider the relevance of two verses from their own cultural heritage to the eighteenth century poem. They have heard, read, written and spoken English. The lesson has been designed to provide a learning experience integrating literature, Jewish sources, language activities and experiential learning of a personal nature. In this it reflects the overall conception of a RICH approach to classroom interactions.

🍎 🍎 🍎

FAMILY ALBUM

Following the success of the original RICH curriculum, the Ministry of Education employed the RICH Staff to write an additional curriculum on Jewish identity, entitled *FAMILY ALBUM: Portraits Drawn from the Life of a People.* Unfortunately, following its completion, it was never published. We are still hopeful that someday this book will make its way off the dusty shelves and into the hands of our young pupils! For now, we will share here our letter to the teachers whom we had hoped would benefit from the book.

Dear Colleague,

FAMILY ALBUM *is a reader for the middle school pupil, society's young adolescents. In his classic book,* Childhood and Society, *Erik Ericson notes that "with the advent of puberty, childhood proper comes to an end. Youth begins." And, it is at this stage of life that the integration of ego identity takes place. A sense of ego identity is defined by Ericson as "the accrued confidence that the inner sameness and continuity prepared in the past are matched by the sameness and continuity of one's meaning for others." In the modern industrialized world, there is a "deep need of youth to redefine its identity."*

In addition to (or as part of) the individual's need to integrate his personal identity, is the issue of group identity, the self-perception of being both whole and part, both independent and an interdependent member of a larger whole.

The authors of FAMILY ALBUM searched for ways in which classroom experiences could help young Israeli adolescent pupils to (a) recognize the sameness and continuity of the collective Jewish past; (b) appreciate how significant they are for their people in the unique historical context; and (c) facilitate the integration of a Jewish national identity.

That search led to FAMILY ALBUM, a collage of Jewish experiences in different times and places. The threads of sameness and continuity of these experiences highlight the significance of Israel and of the homecoming of many members of the family that is the People of Israel.

Obviously, no album can do more than suggest the diversity and sameness of the Jewish past. This book contains portraits from more than twenty communities, ranging from Spain of the eighth century to the drama of "Operation Shlomo"[10] of May 1991. We believe that reading and discussing these texts will be informative and will develop empathy for the difficulties, and pride in the accomplishments of the Family. Knowledge, empathy, and pride are valuable ingredients in the building of identity. Clarifying a shared past may strengthen a sense of shared identity and the dream of a shared future.

FAMILY ALBUM, in the RICH tradition, seeks to take the fullest educational advantage of the hours available to teachers of English. In the RICH tradition too, is the attention paid to language appropriate to pupils' level reflected in the many comprehension

---

[10] A covert Israeli military operation to airlift Ethiopian Jews to Israel in 1991

exercises and in the opportunities presented for listening, speaking, role-playing and discussion. There are suggestions for short written assignments such as letter or journal writing. But the emphasis is on reading comprehension and oral practice. The texts lend themselves to the exploration of meaning on several levels; the events themselves and the significance of each event in terms of the sense of identity of the central figures.

Erikson adds, "The adolescent mind is essentially a mind of...a psychosocial stage between childhood and adulthood, between the morality learned by the child and the ethics to be developed by the adult... The young adult, emerging from the search for identity, is eager and willing to fuse his identity with others... he is ready to commit himself to concrete affiliations and partnerships and to develop the ethical strength to abide by such commitments..."

It is our conviction that educators everywhere must take moral responsibility towards helping adolescents become healthy young adults, comfortable in both their personal and social identity. That conviction informs the concept and pages of FAMILY ALBUM.

How can teachers translate these pages into productive educational classroom experiences? A familiar educational principle is teaching the unknown based on the known. We suggest several strategies:

1. *Note that each portrait is presented in a time and place frame. A text is identified as America 1860's or Germany 1940's... This immediately sets a specific historic and geographic stage for the story to follow. Teachers may add other information or ask questions about that period and place. For example, related to this book's report of Russian migration to America in the 1880's, teachers might profitably refer to other movements of immigration to Palestine.*

   In addition to helping pupils to recognize the multiple roads chosen, many "what if" and "why" questions hover in the air. Teachers, of course, may choose to develop certain issues in more depth or not at all. But the option is there, to be used to the degree individual teachers choose.

2. *The "WH" approach used in the opening lesson is suggested as a running motif throughout the book. The WHERE and WHEN are usually given, but the WHO, WHAT, and WHY illustrate*

repeatedly the "diversity and sameness" of our history. Pupils can be asked periodically to collect, compare and contrast what is happening to whom and possibly consider WHY.

3. As in the RICH books, Hebrew verses are interspersed throughout. These are, as it were, captions for the texts, underlining, emphasizing or simply commenting on the portrait presented through an original Jewish source. This deliberate integration of known (Hebrew) and unknown (new English text) is designed to reinforce the notion of collective past and collective wisdom or experience.

4. Another strategy focuses on the overview of the stream of family history through the inclusion of Recent Developments. These are later "snapshots" of family members met earlier. A striking example is the texts about the Jews of Ethiopia. The authors were delighted to be able to include the historic Operation Shlomo of May 1991 in the book.

   This strategy lends itself to many interesting classroom activities with a future orientation, such as planning pages in the Album on a personal or national level, creating word pictures of desired events, and explaining why they are "desired."

Each of these strategies stems from an acceptance of Ericson's assessment of the "deep need of youth to redefine its identity."

Is Jewish identity in jeopardy today? A July 1991 Newsweek item tells us that in the USA, since 1985, 52% of all marriages involving Jews have been interfaith; in 1964 only 9% were interfaith marriages. Three quarters of the children of interfaith marriages are not raised as Jews... An American Jew comments, "You cannot expect continuity if Jews know little about what they wish to continue!" We dare not be smug about Jewish identity in Israel. Sensitive teaching of FAMILY ALBUM may help our pupils recognize our natural partnership and common identity with the family abroad, past, present, and future.

THE RICH STAFF
June 1992

Teachers respond to RICH

- *It was one of those rare occasions when the whole class shared in our activity. Even the weakest girls understood the issue and were involved. The fact that we spent a whole week on it gave everybody (including myself!) the feeling that we were not just doing ordinary school curriculum.*

- *The classes that have had the privilege of working with RICH have benefited greatly; almost all the pupils prefer these units to any other material they have experienced and I have enjoyed the sharing with them very much.*

- *I like the RICH material very much. It is real enrichment. I could feel that we were learning far more than the English language, and the pupils' reactions were heartwarming.*

- *I put a lot into teaching the RICH program and felt that I received so much in return. It's really made my teaching year.*

- *As an English teacher, I never saw my role as teaching values. Since then, I concentrate on moral issues...RICH is perfect for that – a "textbook" for values!*

Pupils respond to RICH

- *The contents of the program are very interesting because they deal with difficulties that have a place in everyone's life. This refers especially to youths, who are often preoccupied with issues such as identity, choosing among various roads in life, relationships with others and with society, etc.*

- *I'd like to say that this material is outstanding and is welcome. It really made me think! We should see more of its kind.*

- *The class discussions made me start speaking in class... The usual texts are far, far away from me and didn't mean anything.... Just new words.... And this material really made me alive in class.*

- *RICH deals with issues that are very important and interesting and they encourage the pupils to discuss general issues in English, a thing they don't do so often. Expressing themselves, the pupils learn much more than in usual lessons, especially when the subject is relevant and something that touches their own lives and experiences.*

- *I think it was a good idea to ask us to ask adults and parents about their opinion on the subjects and in this way to make them also involved with this material. It's also a good chance for us to hear other opinions.*

Chapter 10
Improving University Instruction

Most of the work of the Center focused on developing significance in schools, elementary through high school. Alongside this work, there were a number of interventions with university faculty that demonstrated the value and relevance of the approach for teaching in universities. The present chapter will describe three such interventions: two at the Hebrew University in Jerusalem (with faculty in the School of Dentistry and the Humanities), and another in one-on-one work with a teacher in an Israeli college.

Building Bridges for Dentists

As director of the Center, I had long hoped for an opportunity to confirm my hunch that the program could be useful for university faculty in general, and in particular for faculty members who had no background in teacher training. We sent a flyer to all the deans offering a course in teaching but got very little response. One inquiry we did receive was from the Dental School of the Hebrew University. A colleague and myself made an hour long presentation to a room filled with white-jacketed men and women who introduced themselves as, "Dani-orthodontistry", "Ruth-gum and root disease", "Peter-bone pathology",etc. Childhood traumas in dental chairs had left their mark on both of us and by the time all twenty introductions had been made, our hearts were pounding with long repressed anxieties. We survived the hour and fled!

In 1987, one of the men in that white circle became the Dean of the School of Dentistry and invited the Center to give a course in teaching to faculty members. In our meeting, we agreed that the course would be offered to interested faculty and would consist of eight five-hour sessions. Ten teachers volunteered to participate; they were men and women ranging in age and experience from mid-thirties to late fifties, from beginning instructors to veteran professors. They came from several different departments and knew each other very casually at best. They had been outstanding students and practitioners, and had been invited to join the faculty over the years. Not one of them had had any formal preparation for the teaching aspects of their roles.

We set the following goals for the course:

1. Participants would clarify the activities their teaching role demanded and consider which skills each activity called for. They would practice those skills systematically and both give and receive feedback.

2. Participants would develop a sense of collegiality and trust that would allow them to perceive the group as supportive enough to entrust with specific personal difficulties in teaching. Time would be spent on helping individual participants solve teaching problems.

3. Participants would consider their collective role as faculty ushering neophytes into a service profession and the larger issues of the social responsibilities inherent in that collective role. They would discuss moral dilemmas practitioners face and consider the possibilities of preparing students to resolve those dilemmas appropriately. They would also discuss moral dilemmas of their teaching role.

In our first session, we defined teaching as "everything a teacher does related to his professional role." Participants were asked to list everything they "do" as teachers, then to share, compare and discuss their lists. This activity generated a collection of teaching skills such as explaining, lecturing, testing, and clinical demonstration on a patient, observation of a student treating a patient, and giving him specific feedback on his performance.

We hoped in this first session to create an atmosphere of collegiality and respect among the participants, and to instill empathy for students and patients. An activity designed to initiate this process is ATTENDING; small groups practicing the ability to maintain eye contact and to exhibit non-verbal interest. Each member of the small group was asked to talk for two minutes about one of his first visits to a dentist. Full attention was paid as each participant recalled their memories of a particular moment in a dentist's chair. They were then asked to present one word that best reflected their feelings about that visit. These words, which were listed on the blackboard, included: FEAR, TENSION, ANXIETY, OK, PANIC, AFRAID, TERRIFIED, CALM, SCARED, and NOTHING SPECIAL.

A question we raised at this point was whether the Dental School took account of the widespread public anxiety about dental care. Was it an issue worth adding to its syllabus? Did they, the faculty, believe future dentists should be prepared to deal with patients' attitudes and fears, and if so, how? A lively and controversial discussion ensued. The next activity was a silent reading of an article dealing with the complexity of the socialization of young professionals and the need for more recognition by professional schools of their responsibility in this process. The text was read and studied using the JIGSAW technique that utilizes peer teaching. The group then analyzed the subject of preparation for the profession: the academic studies, the clinical training, and the learning and internalizing of the norms of the professional culture. Thus ended the first session of the course on university teaching.

The group met for seven more sessions, continuing to move from the practice of specific skills in a microteaching format, to role-playing of a clinical experience, such as giving feedback to a student who has just made a serious mistake, to reading texts relevant to their own professional lives. One such text described the work done at the University of Minnesota to measure the moral sensitivity of dental school students, and how the faculty had responded to the shocking lack of sensitivity the study revealed. This led to a personal inventory of recurring moral dilemmas in dental practice, of how these had been resolved, and again, of the possible implications for teachers of the dental school.

During our eight sessions with these teachers, we had tried to build a bridge, a bridge linking the professional to the teaching role and responsibilities of the course participants. At the last session, we distributed a questionnaire asking for their evaluation of the course in general and of specific elements of the program. The ten participants were asked to rank each topic as *not helpful, helpful, or very helpful.* Not one topic was considered *not helpful* by even one participant. Many topics were ranked as either *helpful or very helpful.* Topics considered *very helpful* by most participants were:

- specifying skills needed for teaching,

- systematic development of teaching skills,

- professional moral dilemmas,

- teaching dilemmas.

The teaching techniques practiced in the course that were most highly valued were SET INDUCTION and GIVING INSTRUCTIONS. Others deemed *very helpful* were:

- small group discussion,

- whole group discussion,

- micro-teaching,

- jigsaw reading and peer teaching of texts.

All ten participants noted the time intensity as very helpful and felt that both social and professional bonding had taken place during the sessions. Overall personal comments were invited at the end of the questionnaire. Following are excerpts from those comments:

- *Excellent! A must once a year.*

- *The process created both an awareness of and an appetite for teaching not felt before.*

- *Time was too short, but I learned about my limitations as a teacher and resolve to improve, using many of the techniques learned in the course.*

- *A real experience! I wish more of our faculty could have the experience of such a course.*

- *I feel a new empathy for our students and have more desire to help them.*

- *An extraordinary experience that will have an impact on my teaching.*

A year later, we found ourselves wondering about the post-course teaching lives of the ten individuals who had formed such a strong and active group. Then we received a telephone call from the new dean of the Dental School informing us that members of his faculty would like to take part in the "teaching experience their colleagues are still talking about." The bridge was still standing!

Workshop for the Humanities Faculty

In 2001, four workshops were ordered for groups of teachers in the Humanities departments. It was our intention that through the workshops, the participants, many of whom placed highest priority on their research, would develop greater appreciation for the importance of teaching, and an increasing sense of responsibility for becoming a better teacher.

The program was therefore designed with the following goals:

1. To create an atmosphere of respect and openness as an implicit model for all learning groups;

2. To enable participants to bring up personal and collective memories of their experiences as students in school and in university;

3. To examine and discuss research that shows correlations between certain behaviors of teachers and the behavioral approaches of students;

4. To structure opportunities for participants to present both successes and failures/problems in their teaching;

5. To define, examine, and practice specific teaching techniques;

6. To initiate the writing of a reflective diary for documenting and evaluating what has been learned;

7. To demonstrate a variety of teaching techniques.

The workshop drew on our work in schools while adapting it to the challenges of university instruction. Issues raised included: What is a "good lesson?" What are my personal goals for a given lesson and what are my expectations for the students at the end of the course? What problems do I face in the classroom, and what new and different teaching skills do I need? Topics were presented in a variety of ways, including work in small groups, group discussion, micro-teaching with video, mini-lectures with group feedback, JIGSAW, etc.

Below are a number of the voices from participants' evaluations at the conclusion of the workshops:

- *I find that the quality of my teaching (over 11 years of experience prior to the workshop) improved greatly. I also enjoy teaching more than ever before.*

- *I learned, I enjoyed, and I was enriched with teaching tools and new ways of thinking about teaching. I am extremely interested in continuing to meet as a means for developing my own teaching to support the development of others.*

- *Looking back on the workshop sessions, I think it was an interesting, intriguing, educational and necessary experience for every teacher. Even though the facilitators lacked expertise in my particular subject area, I found they were extremely sensitive to the nuances of my teaching and to how it could be improved. I found the framework of a workshop conducive to learning, as I learned the most from watching others.*

- *I found it very helpful to meet with the others and to talk about common problems. But most importantly the workshop succeeded in bringing a lot of issues to our awareness, where we could think about them and change them if necessary.*

From Clinic to Workshop to Clinic

As the reader may recall, the experience of working as a Teaching Improvement Specialist in the Clinic of the University of Massachusetts taught me several crucial lessons. First, that Dwight Allen's concept of Teaching as a Craft held true across subject matter and second, that these skills could be identified, analyzed, practiced and improved. As a teacher educator, I wished that we could somehow duplicate this model at my own university in Israel. As an Israeli, I realized that the one-to-one clinic model was obviously a luxury far beyond our means. The determination to find a way to solve this problem led to the development of the Center to improve teaching and to our decades of workshops across the country.

Years after the Center had closed, a friend of mine who was the Dean of a local college shared her concerns about a colleague: "Alex is very serious, a good researcher who has published in his field, is devoted to his profession, and is a committed member of our staff. However, Alex is very unhappy with the students' evaluations of his teaching. He takes his teaching very seriously, prepares each lesson carefully, and cannot understand what is wrong. I remember your stories of the Clinic to Improve University Teaching at Amherst. It would be wonderful if Alex could be helped!"

Alex visited me at home and we talked about his courses, his teaching, and the student evaluations. That was the first of ten or so meetings. Alex, like many of his peers, taught by lecture and assigned readings. He was intrigued by suggestions to dramatically vary teaching style. After describing the unit to be taught, we considered many options as well as the strengths of each for the particular class and content. Should he talk about the reading before the students read it? Should there be small group work after the reading with set questions? Should he ask one student to prepare and present? Should students compose the questions? Perhaps a panel?...

He showed great courage; took a deep breath and taught in ways foreign to his own experiences as student or teacher.

We finished that semester and began to think about a new course for the following year. The pattern continued for several more meetings. The year ended and Alex called me in great excitement. The student evaluations had come in...Alex was voted Best Teacher of the Year!

The circle had closed. The Clinic had gone to Workshop and back to the one-to-one model. And it works in Israel as it worked in Amherst and elsewhere.

Chapter 11
Exercises for Deepening Learning

In previous chapters, we have described some of the basic FORMS developed by Center staff, and we have described their implementation in a variety of settings. In this chapter, we would like to describe additional FORMS and exercises that we often implemented at an appropriate point in the workshops. These will include ATTENDING, PICTURES, MARCHING AND DANCING, a HATFUL OF FEELINGS, and NOSTALGIA.

ATTENDING

One of the first subjects we worked on is that of ATTENDING: Listening wholeheartedly and compassionately to the "other." Many courses world-wide are given on Public Speaking, Oral Expression, Voice Enhancement, and Getting Others to Listen to You. According to Carl Rogers (1983), ATTENDING is a conscious and purposeful activity that exhibits itself verbally and non-verbally through body language. Dwight Allen (1969) maintains that ATTENDING is one of the many teaching skills that can be isolated and broken down into its different parts to be learned, practiced and perfected.

The philosophy of the Center was that both the theory of Carl Rogers, Teacher as Facilitator, and the theory of Dwight Allen, Teacher as Master of Skills, are necessary for good teaching. ATTENDING is a perfect example of how both these theories were put into practice in our workshops.

We usually opened with a personal story with which everyone can identify. For example, who hasn't gone into an office to discuss an issue when the person on the other side of the desk is eating, writing, answering a phone call or looking for something in his drawers while urging us on with our story with, "Go on! Keep talking! I'm listening!" One thing we feel for sure is this person is doing anything BUT listening!

How do we show we are really listening? By silence, not interrupting, and body language, looking directly at the person, leaning forward... Dwight Allen broke down ATTENDING into its different parts that can all be practiced systematically.

The most basic part, Eye Contact, often seems to be the most difficult. One of our staff members related the story of how while she was washing dishes her little girl was telling her about something that happened to her that day. At some point the little girl shouted, "Mummy! You're not listening to me!"

"Of course I'm listening to you!" the mother replied.

"No! You're not listening to me with your EYES!" retorted the girl.

And so, with this story in mind we practice Eye Contact. We emphasize that this is an exercise in a "laboratory"; it is not descriptive of a real-life situation. We ask the members to sit directly opposite each other and to look into each other's eyes for 30 seconds with no verbal expression whatsoever. Stopwatch in hand, we give the signal and the participants have to look into each other's eyes. It always amazes us how difficult this exercise is and how uncomfortable people feel doing this. It is not unusual for pairs to burst into giggles or to just look away. While some participants might feel uncomfortable with this exercise, others from different cultures would find this exercise rude, immodest, or just unacceptable behavior! As workshop leaders we must always be aware of different cultural behaviors and taboos and sometimes we have to skip this exercise altogether.

We always allow a few minutes for reactions to this exercise. In every group, there are always participants who are surprised by how difficult it was for them to look into someone's eyes for 30 seconds! It is always noted how eyes can "say" so much; how just a look of the eye, without uttering a sound, can signal distress, approval, anger, love, shame and so many other emotions.

For the second stage of Dwight Allen's exercise, we ask these same pairs who are sitting opposite each other to practice non-verbal attending. Each member of the pair is asked to talk about a topic for **two** minutes while the listener practices non-verbal attending; that is, eye contact and body language with no verbal interruptions. At the end of two minutes, the speaker gives feedback to his attender; how I felt you were or were not listening to me. The attender now has his turn to speak while his partner practices listening followed by feedback.

The discussion topics are given by the leaders. They are always non-threatening, nostalgic and easy to talk about. For this exercise, the topic is "The Neighborhood Where I Grew Up."

For the next exercise we ask each pair to "take a pair," forming groups of four. We explain that research has shown that teachers in frontal classrooms look mainly to the center and right of the room. One can only imagine how the pupils on the left side of the room feel! In this next exercise, we practice attending by both the speaker and the listeners. The topic for this exercise is "My First Teaching Job." Each member of the foursome speaks for two minutes, remembering to make eye contact with all the listeners while the listeners practice non-verbal attending. The speaker then gives feedback on how she felt all members were listening followed by feedback from the listeners who tell if they got equal eye-contact time. All members of the group practice speaking and listening, always giving each other feedback.

An important side benefit to these exercises is to see how much the members enjoy telling their stories and listening to other stories, often from very different cultural and social backgrounds. They often continue sharing their stories during the breaks, thereby creating a sense of bonding between themselves.

After a short break (which is carefully planned and timed), the members return to the full circle for an open discussion. If the group is large, we form two discussion groups, what we call SPLIT-SCREEN. The group(s) assign a recorder and the question is posed, "How can we improve the attending between teacher and pupil, and between the pupils themselves? How do we get them to listen to each other?" The time limit is announced and at the conclusion, the recorders report on the outcomes of the discussion.

This discussion is followed by the distribution of three excerpts of Carl Rogers' writings on the topic of listening as a deep emotional experience. Depending upon the time, the nature of the group and many other factors, these texts can be studied in pairs or larger groups or in JIGSAW fashion. Members can underline meaningful statements, share personal stories, or relate to the text in other ways.

It is interesting to observe how the behavior of the workshop participants often changes after they have experienced the exercise on ATTENDING. It becomes evident that they are more aware of their listening and attending skills expressed in their body language and non-interruptive behavior. The difference is especially noted in members who were absent from the ATTENDING session.

Often, to add a little spice and charm, or sometimes just to lighten the air after a heavy topic or serious work, we will conclude with an interesting or humorous anecdote or story, or quotation. In this case, we often turn to Rabbi Nachman of Bratslav (an 18th century Hassidic leader):

In our Youth, we learn to speak,
In our Old Age – to be silent.
This is Man's greatest weakness,
He learns to speak before he learns to be silent!

PICTURE ACTIVITIES

A picture activity can be used as a SET INDUCTION for a defined theme. It might also demonstrate an idea or sum up a unit. A visual stimulus is likely to arouse both cognitive and emotional processes of learning and insight. It therefore can serve as an opening for a full group or small group discussion.

For example, the following picture activity can be used for practicing decision-making, compromise, validation and acceptance of others' choices.

Compile a set of beautiful photos of the outdoors: landscapes, mountain and ocean views, flowering gardens, beaches etc. (without the presence of people or animals).

Place them around a large desk or table and ask members to go around the table twice before choosing and picking up their favorite (or second favorite if their favorite has been taken).

In groups of three, explain to each other the reason why the picture you chose is your favorite. After each explanation, the other two partners in the group say one **positive** statement about your choice. This statement must be sincere and relate to a specific detail(s) in the picture.

The entire group stands in one circle, each member displaying his picture. If a member sees his first favorite in the hands of another, he is asked to go over to that person and explain why that picture is really his favorite.

In the whole group, the question is asked, "What did you learn from this activity? What did you learn from being asked to make a positive statement about a picture you did **not** choose?"

As we often do, we ask the members to think about didactic applications of this activity. As a SET INDUCTION for a new topic? Perhaps as a review of a unit in history? nature studies? Each pupil will choose a picture he wants to talk about or that he knows he **can** talk about. What a delightful change from the usual review lessons!

The following SET INDUCTION, for example, can be used to introduce the study of stereotyping in the classroom:

Compile a set of clear photos of unknown faces. While the participants are out on a break, arrange the chairs in groups of three and place one photo on each seat. When the members return, ask each one to share his feelings about his picture. What do you think you know about him/her? professionally? personally?

The leader will then ask the group, "We gave you pictures of perfect strangers and yet you all had something to say. **Why**? What does this say about external looks and first impressions?"

The members are then asked to share in pairs about "a time when my first impression was mistaken." This sharing is followed by an open discussion on: Do teachers discriminate against a child because of his physical appearance? Or, what effect does a child's physical appearance have on the teacher?

There are many research studies on how teachers' use of stereotyping in the classroom affects their attitudes towards their pupils. These can be presented in JIGSAW fashion or as a mini–lecture to be followed by a discussion on: What can teachers do to avoid stereotyping?

MARCHING AND DANCING

In my husband's *Zede*'s (Grandfather's) home, there were two alternate melodies for singing the Psalm preceding the Grace After Meals. One was sweet, slow and lyrical – reminiscent of a waltz. The other resonated with *Zede*'s years as a soldier in Franz Josef's army, having the steady beat and rhythm of a clear military march. Thus, we would turn to each other before Grace, and ask in family code: Waltz or March, which will it be now? Many years into this tradition as I prepared a workshop session, I had a startling insight – Teaching is a marvelous mix of MARCHING and DANCING!

In MARCHING, the emphasis is on keeping in step as everyone moves in the same direction at the same pace. Every teacher knows about MARCHING, having been well trained in the importance of covering the material: all together now, straight to the exam, "Forward march!" to the next item on the curriculum!

DANCING, in contrast, comes in many forms and rhythms – one may dance solo or in pairs, ballroom dancing, wild groups of folk dancing, accompanied by song or instrument. In DANCING with the material, we review, recall, reflect; alone, in pairs, in a large group; as homework or as a group project. The basics of a particular subject studied, whether it be history, science, or sociology, have been acquired; now this knowledge will be turned and twirled, integrated by looking at it from many angles. Our participants know that an item on the board announcing DANCING is sure to be interesting, different and often fun.

An example:

MISS A (described in the Preface) is usually introduced in the first or second session of our workshops. Later on in the year as we discuss the distribution of report cards, we will often write on our MENU - Dancing With Miss A. In this activity, we ask our participants, in pairs, to ROLE PLAY a first grader of Miss A showing his report card to his parent. The parent reacts.

Next is a Replay. We ask the pair to reverse roles and for another twist: The pupil is now a first grader of Miss B (or another teacher if we haven't mentioned Miss B earlier).

In the discussion to follow, we ask the group what emotions were aroused in the pupils of Miss A and Miss B? In the parents? How do these emotions affect the attitude of the pupil toward school? What about the parent/child relationship? And the DANCING goes on...

A HATFUL OF FEELINGS

In this activity, A HATFUL OF FEELINGS, participants are asked to think quietly of problems, dilemmas, topics they would like to be considered in the workshop. A few minutes are given for thinking and writing on small pieces of paper anonymously. A hat is then passed around and participants drop their "feelings" into the hat. At any time during the workshop a "feeling" is randomly selected and read aloud to the group. Depending upon the topic, the group then chooses a method/technique of relating to the issue: brainstorming, group discussion, role playing etc.

Following is a partial list of the contents of one such "Hatful" from the Head Teachers Seminar in January 1986 in England.

Feeling	Suggested Technique
Coping with teachers waiting for retirement	ROLE PLAY
Educating parents to think about their children's education as educators do	GROUP DISCUSSION
Clarifying role of School Governors	GROUP DISCUSSION
Responding to personal requests from Staff that intrude on professional obligations	GROUP DISCUSSION
Clarifying roles/rules of parent helpers in school	SIMULATION
Strategies for dealing with a "Miss Darcy"	ROLE PLAY
Clarifying the role of parents in daily school life	BRAINSTORM
Strategies for "unfreezing" staff before introducing a curriculum or other change	SMALL GROUPS
Fostering self-government and a sense of responsibility and dependability in pupils	BRAINSTORM
Involving parents in secondary school in the field of curriculum options and career choices	ROLE PLAY
Strategies for Staff Development in our schools	SMALL GROUPS

NOSTALGIA

NOSTALGIA refers to individual and group exercises organized around evoking and sharing significant and meaningful memories from different life stages. Nostalgic sharing exercises have included, for example: My first teaching job; Childhood games and songs; Rituals and ceremonies in the school where I learned; Heroes of that school; My first report card; My first job in the work force; My Miss A; or My Miss Darcy; A custom or ritual I took from my parents' house to my own... The list goes on and on.

In many of our workshop activities, we purposely arouse nostalgic memories of the participants as a set induction or as a way to promote sensitivity to a specific topic or issue. Through these activities, we generate exchanges between members that promote a warm and friendly environment that in turn encourage bonding, friendship, and trust.

One of our very first activities in opening a new workshop is Teachers in my Life. Teachers are asked to recall a Good Teacher and describe him/her to the member sitting immediately next to him. In a matter of a few minutes, members who might never have had any discussion with their colleagues have now learned something about each other's past. In addition, we "utilize" their collected descriptions of Good Teachers to initiate the topic of Good Teaching.

In the next workshop, we would probably discuss the issue of ATTENDING. To practice the concept of Real Listening, groups of three are asked to spend two minutes each describing "My Childhood Neighborhood." This activity arouses a lot of enthusiasm and laughter accompanied by lively hand gestures. As workshop leaders who have their fingers on the stopwatch, it is always hard to stop them in the middle of these exchanges. But stop we must and these warm exchanges often continue into the breaks. It has happened on more than one occasion that teachers of different ages find they come from the same town, city or school! Different cultures meet and mix as "neighborhoods" from all over the world come together creating a kind of ethnic melting pot!

The powerful impact nostalgic exercises have on the group cannot be overemphasized. However, as educational facilitators, we always have to be sensitive to the potential risks of NOSTALGIA. One such case occurred when the group was asked to share their childhood neighborhoods. A strained quiet voice was heard, "But my childhood neighborhood was **Auschwitz!**" (to which we responded by asking her if there was something she wished to tell her partner about her Auschwitz childhood or perhaps she just wished to listen to her partner's recollections.)

Another poignant example occurred when a group was asked to write about "A Nurturing Environment at a Specific Time in My Life." One of the participants was visibly having difficulty and seemed uncomfortable. Later, when the group was asked to respond to the activity, this member reported that at a difficult time in her life, she did **not** have the nurturing environment she badly needed. But focusing on writing about it made her realize the good that she did have! It made her feel better about her past. The powers of remembering!

On July 8, 2013, many years after the Center was closed, an article about the powers of Nostalgia appeared in *The New York Times.* Below is a small excerpt from the article written by John Tierney:

After a decade of study...by dozens of researchers around the world... nostalgia has been shown to counteract loneliness, boredom, and anxiety. It makes people more generous to strangers and more tolerant of outsiders. Couples feel closer and look happier when they're sharing nostalgic memories. On cold days, or in cold rooms, people use nostalgia to literally feel warmer...The net effect is to make life seem more meaningful...when people speak wistfully of the past, they typically become more optimistic and inspired about the future... "Nostalgia serves a crucial existential function," Dr Clay Routledge, a psychologist at North Dakota State University, says. "It brings to mind cherished experiences that assure us we are valued people who have meaningful lives."

Chapter 12
Topics for Developing Significance

In the course of our work, we identified a number of topics whose understanding was critical for becoming significant educators. For each of these we presented relevant research, and designed processes through which workshop participants could internalize the findings and discover their relevance to their own work in schools. This chapter will present three of these topics: SCHOOL CULTURE, WORK, and HUMOR in the classroom.

School Culture

Building strong school cultures is ultimately tied to improving educational performance.

(Deal and Kennedy; Educational Leadership Feb 1983)

"Different Strokes for Different Folks" was the name of a very popular American TV situation comedy that portrayed the lives of two families of completely different cultural backgrounds living next door to each other. As they befriend each other, it becomes clear, in a humorous way, that the customs of one are totally foreign and even unacceptable to the other!

"Different Rules for Different Schools" might be another title for our unit on SCHOOL CULTURE, which we usually introduce with a personal story or anecdote that ends with someone saying, "That's not the way we do things around here!" or "That's the way it's done here." After mentioning more examples of different norms and behaviors among different sectors of society, we ask our participants to think back to a time when they were members of a specific group, perhaps a youth movement, sports club, or a volunteer organization. We them ask them to recall a certain norm or behavior which was "the way it was done,"

Roland Barth's definition of Culture (Barth, 1990). In pairs, they each share one memory.

Moving from personal life to school life, we list on the board the six elements that together create a school culture (Deal, 1978). Briefly explained:

1) Shared values and beliefs: The agreed upon values and beliefs of the school have to be clear to the student, staff and parent body whether it be educational, social or extra-curricular.

2) Rituals: Things done regularly, such as bells, prayers, breaks, meetings.

3) Ceremonies: Episodic occasions, graduations, holiday celebrations, awards, assemblies, which provide tangible opportunities for values to be reinforced, heroes to be celebrated, symbols displayed.

4) Heroes: The figures in the school or society who embody the values of the school. Heroes can be from the past as well as from the present.

5) Stories: These stories of the school illustrate to all the school's values and heroes.

6) Gossips: In a variety of ways, gossips continue to spread the word of, "How things are done around here."

Participants are asked to think back to their school days and to choose **one** of the six elements that was important in their school. In groups of three, one by one, they will share their memories of how that element was felt by the students, and what values were being conveyed.

As we do often, we might ask the group for any SPECIALS heard in the small groups. These SPECIALS often add spice to the discussions and foster cohesiveness among the group members.

Moving on to My School Today we ask our participants to think of the school where they teach today, and to list everything that comes to mind which fits into these six categories.

They are then asked to sit in groups of five and discuss which elements are most strongly felt in their school and how. It is interesting to note that even when all participants of the workshop are from the same school there is not always unanimous agreement!

Next comes the hard part. Members are asked to choose **one** element that is not clearly felt, and to plan ways in which to strengthen it in the school. This might require more than the time allotted in the workshop setting, so future meetings might be scheduled. One person from each group of five is asked to record the conclusions of this discussion and to read them aloud to the whole group.

We ask for one volunteer to collate and organize these brief reports to be distributed to all members. We express the hope that we will be hearing about ECHOES from this activity in the very near future!

ö ö ö

An ECHO from the FIELD - Chava Zohar

In the years following the mass Russian immigration to Israel, a principal of a school in Jerusalem noticed that the teachers who had come from Russia perceived teacher-student relations in a way that was radically different from the reality of Israeli school culture. For example, one of the teachers complained that a student approached him, patted him on his arm and said, "Today's lesson was very good." The teacher had responded angrily that he - as the teacher - is not the student's friend or colleague and should be treated with respect!

The principal therefore ordered a workshop to clarify the school culture and suggest strategies to help them adapt to their new role at school.

There was a lot of frustration at the beginning of the workshop, which expressed itself in a lot of criticism of student behavior, the lack of discipline in the school, and low academic standards. We encouraged participants to describe specific cases and to use them as opportunities to consider seriously how teacher-student relations differ in various cultures.

At the conclusion of the last workshop one teacher announced, "You have done a Perestroika for us!"[11]

ö ö ö

---

[11] The policy of economic and governmental reform instituted by Mikhail Gorbachev in the Soviet Union during the 1980's.

Work

We are all familiar with Snow White's seven little dwarfs who go off to work early each morning, pick axes in hand, singing joyfully, "Hi Ho, Hi Ho, it's off to work we go..."

Do we all feel like singing "Hi Ho...." when we go off to work each morning? After this opening, we (the workshop leaders) distribute a handout of different thoughts on the idea of Work expressed by different authors and philosophers throughout different periods:

1. *The ultimate object of work is leisure.* (Aristotle)

2. *Work is the central activity by which individuals give meaning to their lives.* (Sigmund Freud)

3. *Every man's work is always a portrait of himself.* (Samuel Butler)

4. *Let us be grateful to Adam. He cut us out of the blessing of idleness and won us the curse of labor.* (Mark Twain)

5. *I don't like work – no man does – but I like what is in work – the chance to find yourself, your own reality – for yourself, not for others – what no man can ever know.* (Joseph Conrad)

6. *It is in work that human beings develop and affirm their personality. When man is no longer responsible for his work, he feels spiritually outraged.* (Jacques Elul)

7. *The most dangerous threat hanging over American society is the threat of leisure.* (Arthur Schlesinger)

8. *We go to work to get the dough to get the food to get the strength to go to work.* (Industrial Workers of the World)

Members of the group are asked to read and study silently and to choose **one** statement that they identify with or agree/disagree with. In pairs, members are asked to share their chosen statements, giving examples. Meanwhile, the leader writes the numbers of the statements on the board in a column. Then, going in order around the room, the leader marks the selection of each participant giving a visual picture of the selections of the group, noting which are the more or less popular choices. The leader might ask for one "representative" of each statement to elaborate to the entire group or perhaps just to choose the most popular or least popular thought. This activity always invites lively discussion and expression of opposing views.

We then advance from personal impressions to the cognitive or academic aspect of the subject. Members read a relevant text for silent individual study (we often use an excerpt from E.F. Schumacher's book *Good Work*). They are asked to underline three sentences that seem most relevant, important, or thought provoking; then to choose **one** to share with their neighbors based on personal experiences.

This activity is followed by the distribution of a second excerpt for silent study. While the members are reading, the leader writes **two** sentences from this text on the board. In groups of **three**, members are asked to recall the experience of someone they know which relates to one of these sentences. By this time, members have reflected on the idea of Work, examined closely their exchanged ideas with their peers, read about the topic and broadened their own knowledge on the subject.

Back to full circle, we ask for reactions, comments and questions on the topic of Work and Work as teachers/principals.

We conclude with Looking Ahead – the impact of our work today on the future with a well-known story from the Talmud[12]:

> The King Adrianus was on his way with his troops to fight another country that rebelled against him. On the way, he saw an elderly man planting fig trees. Adrianus asked the elderly man how old he was, to which the old man replied, "One hundred years, Your Majesty."
>
> Shocked, Adrianus exclaimed, "You're a hundred years old and you're planting fig trees! Why do you labor so? You won't live long enough to enjoy the fruits of those trees!"
>
> The old man replied, "Your Majesty, Just as my Forefathers labored for my benefit, so will I labor for the benefit of my descendants!"

---

[12]The collection of ancient Rabbinic writings consisting of the Mishna and the Gemara, the basis of religious authority in Orthodox Judaism.

Humor

In 1994, a super-sized headline appeared on page 11 of the popular Israeli newspaper *Maariv.* In quotation marks it screamed, *"Teachers in Israel Have No Sense of Humor!"* The article went on to describe a study conducted by Professor Adir Cohen of the School of Education of Haifa University in which he found that students who study in an environment that includes humor are much more likely to attain better grades. They also have a better rate of success in subjects demanding abstract learning such as mathematics. According to Professor Cohen, only a small percentage of teachers were found to have a sense of humor or to use humor in the classroom. "If only the educational system appreciated the power of the use of humor in the classroom, in relation to curriculum and student-teacher relationships, it would be possible to effect dramatic and significant changes in education in Israel!" concluded Professor Cohen.

Spurred on by this dramatic article, we decided to construct a unit on HUMOR IN THE CLASSROOM. We open with an old folk tale, which goes something like this: At the time of Creation, God gave unique gifts to each animal. To the kangaroo, He gave a pouch, to the peacock, a multi-colored tail, to the canary a magnificent voice and so on. After a while, God realized He forgot to give a special gift to the human. So He gave the humans the best gift of all: a sense of humor! Which turned out to be such an important feature of our development, our personalities, our character, in essence, our humanism! Just think! The first voluntary act a human baby does besides cry for food is smile! And how that smile melts hearts even of stone!

These few statements always elicit fervent responses from our group including personal stories of the role Humor plays in our lives, or how Humor saved the day in particular situations. After allowing for a few such reactions, we continue by distributing a handout of eight statements titled THOUGHTS on HUMOR noting the time span and the diversity of the speakers:

1. *Laughter results from a mixture of joy and shock.* (Rene Descartes)

2. *Laughter is a kind of sudden glory which we achieve by observing the weaknesses of others and comparing them with our own strengths.* (Thomas Hobbes)

3. *Laughter comes when two or more inconsistent happenings are united into one.* (James Beattie)

4. *The invisible source of humor lies not in joy but in sadness. There is no humor in Paradise.* (Mark Twain)

5. *Man alone suffers so terribly in the world that he had to invent laughter.* (Friedrich Nietzche)

6. *Laughter is a sense of freedom from the limitations of the real world.* (Dugas)

7. *Humor is a triumph of the pleasure-principle over painful reality. It turns an event that would cause suffering into one less significant. Humor helps man to cope with tension.* (Sigmund Freud)

8. *Laughter is the jolly policeman who keeps the social traffic going in the right ways.* (Wallis)

Statements can be handled in a number of ways. Each person chooses one he agrees or disagrees with and shares with a neighbor. Or a "vote" can be taken in the group with the results written on the board. One representative of the two most voted for statements explains. Another option is setting up a PANEL, each panelist explaining and/or relating the chosen statement to a personal experience.

At this point, we present a MINI-LECTURE on the necessity of humor for good mental health based on our readings of some of the psychological literature.[13] All the studies we read concluded that humor is absolutely necessary for good mental health. Humor contributes to pleasure; it elevates us from depression and can ease stressful times by providing an escape. Humor also offers an acceptable way of expressing anger or frustration. In addition, humor can lighten a difficult or uncomfortable situation. It is no wonder that comedies are the most popular TV shows.

Yaakov Kirschen, an Israeli political cartoonist, had this to say about his job[14]:

My job as a cartoonist is to tell the truth as I see it. The truth in many cases is hard to take and painful.

---

[13] One book we used was *Humor: Its Origin and Development* by Paul E. McGhee (1979)

[14] Yaakov Kirschen, ISRAEL SCENE MAGAZINE (June 1980)

There are two ways that society sets people up to tell the truth. The first way is a Jewish invention – the Prophet. The Prophet comes out in the street and says, "Hey! The King is doing us wrong!" Sometimes, they would kill the prophet. In Europe, they figured out a better system for the Prophet. He'd put on funny clothes and bells, and run around and fall on his face, and was called a Jester. Then in the middle of all this slapstick, he was allowed to say, "Hey! The King is doing us wrong!"

Today, we don't have prophets and we don't have jesters, but we do have comedians and cartoonists. I'm a cartoonist and when I do a cartoon I make it so that you laugh, and when you laugh, like the King who laughs at the Jester, you're able to see the truth and not feel the sting so much.

In pairs, we ask our participants to tell each other of a time when Humor eased a stressful situation or enabled someone to "see the truth and not feel the sting." After five minutes of sharing, we ask the group if anyone heard a special story. There always are special stories to be heard.

Having been sensitized to the positive influence of humor in their lives, the participants can now progress to thinking about the function of humor in their classrooms. In the days of yore, humor was used in a cynical fashion to discipline children. A pupil who misbehaved was put in the corner and forced to wear a Dunce Cap or Donkey Ears, while all the children laughed at him. Today we know how harmful this method was. But humor can actually encourage better behavioral and academic performance. According to the studies we read, the answer is an overwhelming "yes!" The educational and psychological literature is abundant with different studies of how the use of jokes or amusing slides enhances learning and desired behavior. How much humor is appropriate and when can Humor be disruptive are questions without clear-cut answers. Each teacher, each class has different needs.

We then ask everyone to organize themselves into groups of five and we present the assignment: Help each other to plan a lesson interspersed with humor taking into consideration the expected pitfalls and difficulties. Group planning in this case is especially helpful for those of us who are "bad at telling jokes." Every member of the small group will leave with an outline for a lesson plan to be tried out in real time in the field! During this working time, gales of chuckling and laughter reverberate around the room. We, the workshop leaders, are sure we're missing out on many a good joke!

Before concluding, we ask the small groups to return to the large group and ask for reactions. Enthusiasm and excitement for this new tool are reported, but there are always expressions of skepticism and fear of trying out something new. It amazes us how group members are always encouraging and supportive of their less courageous peers.

We can't wait for the next session to hear their ECHOES FROM THE FIELD!

Chapter 13
Codes for Facilitators

In the course of the work of Center staff, a number of codes were developed to help staff members to navigate in complex situations. These codes became a kind of secret language, helping staff communicate in shorthand. They became very helpful in planning and reviewing, acting as a kind of checklist for the facilitator who needs to bring all the many pieces together to form a coherent whole. In this chapter we will describe three of these codes: SPECIAL (used for planning and evaluating sessions), CREASIS (used to guide role plays), and the FIVE–TIONS (used in preparing for a difficult meeting).

SPECIAL

SPECIAL (Social, Sharing, Secret, Personal, Experiential, Empathy, Communication, Connectedness, Introspection, Attending, Awareness, Learning) is one of our basic codes, reminding us of essentials in planning for a session.

Many of our FORMS are SOCIAL, from Hello Who is Here on the MENU, to MISSING, to working in pairs. All small group work is considered SHARING on different levels that are determined by the workshop leader's perception of the needs of the group, the readiness to share, the relevance of the overall unit, etc. SECRET refers to secret writing, often suggested during a session, to encourage both reflection and totally open private writing, which may or may not be invited later on. The writings are, of course, relevant to the topic of the session. For example, Symptoms of Burnout in my Professional Life, or Three Wishes I have for the Staff Room, or Changes in Schedule.

PERSONAL is a pivotal element of Center work. Many sharings are personal. MEMBER is deeply personal. Our work is often EXPERIENTIAL and structured to practice for EMPATHY. ROLE PLAY is a form that is helpful for this purpose as we can create any problematic school issue and ask one participant to be the veteran teacher and to attend to and respond to the new younger colleague's stress.

Many of our classic FORMS encourage if not demand COMMUNICATION and CONNECTEDNESS. An important stage in any session is INTROSPECTION, during which people are given opportunities, as in the secret writing, to spend time looking inward to explore how they feel and what they think about a particular situation or issue. Introspection followed by ATTENDING to the other leads to a broadened AWARENESS. Finally, we make sure that there is LEARNING of several kinds, including academic content of a study or text, or a research finding.

Later, at the end of the day, or week, we review what we actually did and consider whether the sessions have been SPECIAL.... We hope so!

CREASIS

CREASIS is a checklist of one of the most important tools in the Center's repertoire. ROLE PLAY, a four to five minute exercise, involves two people in a discussion on a pre-assigned topic where each participant acts out a certain role. Pairs in the workshops are asked to sit directly opposite each other to maximize eye contact and before they begin, they are reminded to demonstrate good ATTENDING skills. The subject or issue is announced as well as the roles of each partner. At the signal, the participants begin their discussion aware of the exact time limit. At the conclusion, the workshop leader might ask for reactions from one of the players. This is often followed by reversing the roles by the participants and then doing a replay so participants can experience both sides of an argument or issue.

An example: A situation to be discussed: A teacher/parent faces his/her student/child who is trying to decide whether or not to become a teacher. The participants of each pair can decide who will take which role. The workshop leader then drops the other shoe by adding the fact that the parent is trying to encourage the child to take up teaching. "You have four minutes. Begin!"

After the exact time given, the workshop leader might ask the children/students what reasons they were given for studying teaching. Were they convincing? Why or why not? What was missing?

To make this exercise more interesting and enriching, the leader will ask the pairs to stay seated and re-discuss the same issue but with a twist. The roles are to be reversed with the parent becoming the child and vice versa. This time the parent/teacher is trying to **dis**courage the child from studying teaching! The same time limit is given and the same questions are asked to the group afterwards.

After eight minutes of role-playing and perhaps another five to ten minutes of group discussions, the participants of the workshop have examined from just about all points of view the rewards and frustrations, the satisfactions and difficulties, the delights and dilemmas of the teaching profession. Or, in other words, they have, in fact, experienced CREASIS:

- Comprehension
- Creativity
- Review
- Rehearsal
- Empathy
- Awareness
- Set induction
- Introspection
- Imagination
- Stretching

Comprehension: There is a story of a young girl who decided to take swimming lessons. The first lessons were devoted to the physics of swimming, keeping the human body afloat and moving in the water in a systematic fashion while not sinking. The girl excelled in her lessons and the day arrived when she felt ready to put her knowledge to the test. With great confidence, she submerged herself into the water only to find herself virtually helpless. She was forced to cling to the sides of the pool for dear life! Upon seeing this, her instructor expressed complete bewilderment! Her response was, "Well, in **theory** I can swim very well!"

And that's the *role* of ROLE PLAY. To examine our initial comprehension of a topic by jumping straight into the unknown waters! And we do so without fear of drowning because we are only "submerged" for two minutes!

Creativity: Although we are given specific roles to play, we are encouraged to think out of the box in a completely non-judgmental atmosphere. Sometimes we even surprise ourselves with our spontaneous creative responses!

Review: As a high school student, Aviva remembers very well thinking, "Tomorrow I can cut class because the teacher is only reviewing the material. BORING!!" Today she thinks how exciting these review lessons could have been. Imagine role playing two sides of the capital punishment debate, the Jews of Spain arguing about becoming Morranos, to declare or not declare a Jewish State in 1948, the abortion-pro-life issue, Socialism vs. Capitalism, the Jews in the desert discussing building the Golden Calf, the Civil War... the possibilities are endless!

Rehearsal: The motto of the Boy/Girl Scouts in the USA: *Always be prepared!* which translated means: make sure you have all the necessary equipment for any situation. In our workshops, "equipment" takes on a different meaning. It includes predicting the nature and all possible outcomes of a certain discussion/meeting, displaying EMPATHY and AWARENESS, and maintaining calm and self-control even in a difficult or unpleasant situation - a tall order indeed. But by practicing and rehearsing through ROLE PLAY all possible aspects of a specific situation, we can enter troubled waters, perhaps with trepidation, but at least we can feel well prepared.

Set Induction: What better SET INDUCTION can there be for introducing a many sided issue than placing participants in a situation they may or may not agree with! If we are not sympathetic to a role we are asked to take, ROLE PLAY will push us to be.

Introspection: ROLE PLAY pushes us into examining just **why** we feel the way we do and explaining our thoughts and opinions not only to our partner but to ourselves as well.

If we disagree with the role we are asked to take, we will have to exercise IMAGINATION and STRETCHING in order to execute our task. After four minutes of sometimes heated role-playing, we are asked to stop mid-sentence. But all our feelers are out and activated, ready to absorb whatever is coming next!

THE FIVE –TIONS (pronounced *shuns*)

The FIVE –TIONS (Validation, Clarification, Consideration, Cooperation and Coordination) is a unique five-step plan specially designed for problematic meetings between two parties where there likely would be confrontation perhaps including hostility. Anyone in the world of teaching can attest to those "butterflies-in-the-stomach" feelings preceding difficult meetings with parents of problematic pupils, or with colleagues or superiors concerning disputed work or professional issues, to name a few. The goals of this plan are to supply tools for diffusing anger or frustration while at the same time displaying understanding and empathy; and for creating a positive non-threatening environment enabling creativity and problem solving. The FIVE -TIONS is an effective tool which, when executed with self-control and patience, can yield satisfying results.

The FIVE -TIONS consist of the following steps, which admittedly are not as easy as they look. We will describe them briefly and then discuss practicing them.

1. *Validation*: An opening remark expressing appreciation for the fact that the meeting is actually taking place. ("Thank you for taking time to meet with me. This matter is of great importance.")

2. *Clarification*: An objective description of the situation giving full details. The goal of this step is to be certain that the problem is very clearly defined.

3. *Consideration*: Besides the objective description of the situation, there are other factors to be taken into consideration; they might be emotional (on both sides), economic, or social. There might be pre-existing realities or other more urgent matters, all of which should be discussed.

4. *Cooperation*: Following the clarification and consideration of all the different aspects of the problem, the questions of cooperating to solve the problem can be raised: "What is our common goal?" "What can each one of us do?" "Let's think

together how we can solve this." "What do you think should be the first thing we do?"

5. *Coordination*: This final stage should include planning the details of ideas which were discussed in step #4, the time-table, others to be involved, methods of communication and follow-up, and the next meeting for evaluation.

In our workshops, we introduce and practice this tool in different ways. Sometimes, we use ROLE PLAY as a SET INDUCTION (one of the S's in CREASIS). We ask two volunteers to role-play a meeting between a frustrated teacher and an angry parent to discuss a specific problem. (It is interesting to note how the "actors" will play their roles to the fullest presenting a lot of anger and hostility!) The other members of the group act as observers who are asked for their comments following the role-play.

We suggest that this meeting could have been conducted differently, and introduce and explain the FIVE-TION Plan. This takes some time but then we are ready for the two "R's" of CREASIS: REVIEW and REHEARSAL. The group is divided into pairs; each pair is given a particular situation, such as:

*   A meeting between a teacher and a parent of a child who is not working up to his potential. The meeting was initiated by the teacher.

*   A meeting between a subject teacher and the *Mechanech*. The subject teacher feels the *Mechanech* is not strict enough and is not consistent and too laid back in disciplining the class. The meeting was initiated by the subject teacher.

*   A meeting between a teacher and a parent of a child who works satisfactorily but feels unappreciated and disliked by the teacher. The meeting was initiated by the parent.

Following the ROLE PLAY, feedback from the person invited to the meeting is given to the initiator of the meeting. Suggested questions to relate to: Did the initiator show understanding and empathy? Did the initiator utilize the Five Steps? How did you feel it? Were you satisfied with the results?

The initiator is asked to reflect on his/her ability to carry through the Five Steps. Were they helpful? How? Were you satisfied with the results? If you did a "replay", would you change anything? Why?

As is often done in our workshops, we ask the whole group for reactions to this activity which often results in further discussion where everyone can benefit from the lively exchange of ideas and experiences.

If time (and stamina!) allow, we then ask the pairs to think of a difficult meeting they might have to participate in sometime in the near future. Together, they plan the FIVE-TIONS, writing specific statements and questions. When possible, at some later date we ask for willing participants to share their experiences of their FIVE –TION meetings (ECHOES from the FIELD).

An ECHO from the FIELD - Aviva Pinchuk

A number of years ago an educator I know had to meet with a very hostile parent. This was a parent known as a troublemaker and naturally, he was very nervous about the results of this meeting. In preparation, the day before the meeting, we practiced the FIVE -TIONS together. Terrified but armed with this new tool, he very anxiously went off to work hoping to survive the day. I was concerned myself! Later that afternoon I jumped when the phone rang. The voice just yelled, "It worked! It worked!"

Chapter 14
The Echo Trail

Growing up in America, I was intrigued by the stories overheard about the Appalachian Trail. It seemed so mysterious and somehow romantic to set off on a long journey on foot, evidently in the wilds. Decades later, I came to know of the Israel Trail and saw, up close, the passionate commitment to Walking the Trail. On those real trails there are special color markers one must look for to make sure that you are on the right track, going in the right direction, moving ahead ... On the ECHO TRAIL, the echoes themselves are the markers, and they show us where our ideas and FORMS have traveled.

Given our primary goal of helping schools to be better places for all who live in them, every form we use and every activity we plan is designed to be taken home to the classroom, to be an agent of change in the culture and atmosphere of that classroom or staff room. Thus, for all of us on staff, an ECHO brought in by participants is a marker of the impact of our work, validation that we are on the right track.

We have noted how popular the simple FORMS of MENU and MISSING are and how powerful MEMBER has proven. Now, we invite you to join us as we follow the remarkable trail of a particular ECHO, as it turned and twisted on its journey.

We read the following poem:

WHAT IF

Shel Silverstein

Last night, while I lay thinking here,
Some Whatifs crawled inside my ear
And pranced and partied all night long
And sang their same old Whatif song:
Whatif I'm dumb in school?

Whatif they've closed the swimming pool?
Whatif I get beat up?
Whatif there's poison in my cup?
Whatif I start to cry?
Whatif I get sick and die?
Whatif I flunk that test?
Whatif green hair grows on my chest?
Whatif nobody likes me?
Whatif a bolt of lightning strikes me?
Whatif I don't grow taller?
Whatif my head starts getting smaller?
Whatif the fish won't bite?
Whatif the wind tears up my kite?
Whatif they start a war?
Whatif my parents get divorced?
Whatif the bus is late?
Whatif my teeth don't grow in straight?
Whatif I tear my pants?
Whatif I never learn to dance?
Everything seems swell, and then
The nighttime Whatifs strike again!

We consider the implications in real life of the speaker's anxieties...some so far- fetched.We invite individual Secret Writing, a private What If in my teaching life...

We share these in pairs, explaining, elaborating, considering options.

We invite any Whatif willing to be shared, and options raised in pair conversation.

We note how the poem was a SET INDUCTION for our own reflection on possible anxieties and dangers in our school lives, how we shared these and went on to consider possible responses if they ever became real. This is classic structured professional reflection.

Now come with us to see what a marvelously creative teacher did with this unit in her second grade classroom!

The children were asked to think of a personal problem, fear or anxiety and write it in a short letter to a class friend. Each child wrote and gave his letter to a friend, and then each child was asked to write a very short clear answer of advice to the friend who wrote. Here are some examples of their work, in school, mid-second grade!

DEAR LILY, WHAT IF THE SCHOOL BURNT DOWN? MAYA

DEAR MAYA. IF THE SCHOOL BURNT DOWN, THE FIRE DRILL WOULD RING AND THERE WOULD BE TEACHERS ALL AROUND THE SCHOOL. AND REMEMBER THE DRILL, LINE UP QUIETLY IN THE HALLS AND WE'LL BE OUT.

DEAR MAYA, WHAT IF WHEN I AM LOOKING AT A DINOSAUR BOOK THEY JUMP OUT OF THE BOOK?

DEAR LILY, THAT IS NOT LIKELY TO HAPPEN, BUT IF IT DID HAPPEN, CLOSE THE BOOK. FROM MAYA

DEAR DORIS, WHAT IF MY DOG FLUFFY DIES AND I HAVE NO PET TO PLAY WITH? I AM WORRIED ABOUT THAT. YOUR FRIEND JUSTIN

DEAR JUSTIN, I UNDERSTAND YOU DON'T WANT FLUFFY TO DIE. I DON'T EITHER. HE IS REALLY CUTE...BUT IF HE DOES, I WILL GET YOU ANOTHER DOG JUST LIKE FLUFFY. SINCERELY, DORIS

DEAR JUSTIN, WHAT IF A CAR WILL RUN OVER MY MOM AND KAREN AND MAYBE DANA TOO? FONDLY DORIS

DEAR DORIS, I THINK I UNDERSTAND YOU DON'T WANT YOUR FAMILY TO BE RUN OVER. TEACH YOUR FAMILY GOOD SAFETY RULES AND TELL THEM TO BE CAREFUL,   YOUR FRIEND JUSTIN

DEAR TALIA, WHAT IF RUTI GETS SICK AND WE HAVE TO HAVE A SUBSTITUTE TEACHER FOR THE REST OF THE YEAR? SHOSHANA

DEAR SHOSHANA, IF RUTI GETS SICK FOR THE REST OF THE YEAR, THEN JUST PRETEND THAT THE SUBSTITUTE IS YOUR REAL TEACHER AND TREAT HER NICELY, FROM TALIA

DEAR MARK, WHAT IF I DON'T GET A GOOD GRADE IN MATH SUBTRACTION? FROM DANIEL

DEAR DANIEL, I THINK THAT YOU SHOULD WORK HARDER IN MATH SUBTRACTION AND DO A LITTLE EVERY DAY, FROM MARK

DEAR JANE, WHAT IF ON FRIDAY, WHEN I SEE MY DAD, HE WILL BE MAD AT ME FOR TELLING MY MOM WHAT HAPPENED IN THE CAR POOL? PLEASE GIVE ME A SOLUTION, THANK YOU FOR YOUR COOPERATION, YOUR BEST FRIEND, SUZIE

DEAR SUZIE, IF ON FRIDAY WHEN YOUR DAD SEES YOU HE GETS MAD AT YOU, TELL HIM TO TALK ABOUT IT RATHER THAN FIGHTING ABOUT IT, YOUR BEST FRIEND JANE

We were given a full marvelous book of these "What Ifs" which we prize...What an ECHO! This teacher took her reflective experience back to school and introduced her young pupils to a reflective and responsive experience of their own. Note the range of their concerns, from the fanciful dinosaur attack to the father's anger at something told to mother to poor grades to teacher illness, etc.

We love ECHOES, and we walk the ECHO TRAIL happily.

Chapter 15
Echoes from Center Staff and School Principals

Chava Greenberg, Center staff

I vividly remember our first meeting. Ora had assembled 15 experienced teachers, none of whom knew one another. On the board, she wrote: TEACHING MATTERS. Of course, it was ambiguous; it could refer to matters related to teaching. But it became immediately clear to us that for Ora it meant that teaching means something, that it is significant. This was one of her slogans.

The first task was to get these 15 people working together, and Ora did this with her carefully planned strategies. She had exercises in which she got us to work in pairs, in fours, sharing personal memories related and unrelated to teaching. With time, the group congealed. We liked each other and wanted to be there. We felt it was important and that what we were learning would be helpful in our teaching.

The sessions took place over the course of an academic year. We were very happy to be together, but we were especially happy with what we were learning. Ora would always start with some cognitive content, with an article or a topic, which we would read and discuss in small groups. Everything Ora did was a teaching skill that could be replicated with teachers or in the classroom. We would divide into small groups and read in turn paragraph by paragraph, then explain and discuss. When we got to the end of a session she would always ask, "What did we do here? What did you learn?" We were always practicing skills and dissecting our experience.

We had a great time that year going through her topics and methods, reading the practice-related literature she recommended, and growing closer as a group. Toward the end of the year, she told us the time had come to begin preparing for our first assignments the following year as staff in the new Center for Staff Development.

We were terrified! We asked ourselves, Ora, and one another: "Wait, there must be a mistake here. We can't do it. Only Ora can do it!" It was then that we made the fortuitous decision that we would go out in pairs so that we could support one another. My first assignment was with the teachers in the Nursing School in Hadassah Hospital. I remember that before our first session in the field, we all had a session with Ora, where we talked about what has to happen in the first meeting and what we would do to make it happen. In small groups, we set up a schedule and rehearsed our roles. Ora was forever encouraging us that we could do it, we were teachers and we knew what teachers needed. All the while, she was modeling how to plan, how to encourage, and how to listen to teachers' voices.

Terrified, Chava Zohar and I went out to meet the nursing teachers, an impressive group of professional women. We went through our paces, left time for feedback from groups, and lo and behold, we were a hit! They had never experienced anything like it. They were particularly curious about the dynamics of co-facilitation. As Ora did with us, we took them BACKSTAGE: "Okay, this is what we did today. How does it fit in with your teaching a classroom of nursing students?" As often happens in such meetings they raised some of the ethical dilemmas they faced, with questions like what to do if this or that happens. We of course did not have the answers but the questions aroused important and interesting group discussion.

So we had an encouraging start. Although we had not been aware of it, we were extremely well prepared. The next time we met as a group we all reported, and mostly all of the pairs had done well. We felt we were on our way.

We met weekly over the many years that the Center operated. Every week Ora brought new material, new topics to think about, or new methods to practice. In addition, we were always eager to report from the field, to explore together why some things did not work, to share our HIGHLIGHTS and celebrate our successes. By listening to one another, we gained perspective on the process. When things were not going well we knew we were not the only ones having trouble. We learned that there were ups and downs in the process but in most cases there was positive progress over time.

We also had practice sessions, sometimes using a camera to practice micro-teaching. If we learned a new method, we would try it out on each other, one or two of us playing the group facilitators and the rest of us playing the teachers. For example, if we had just learned how to teach teachers to give directions and I was chosen to be the group leader, I had to write out the directions for something I knew very well (e.g. a cake I know how to bake, a route I know how to take to a chosen location) and then present them to the class using the guidelines Ora had provided. Sometimes we filmed the interaction so we could look at ourselves and analyze our own behaviors. Ora was always encouraging, but we were subjected to the reactions of our peers – who of course had been taught how to give constructive feedback.

Every session was a learning session as well as a bonding session. We made friendships, worked together with our co-facilitators (always meeting in person to prepare workshops), and always prepared thoroughly. Of course, some schools were less than satisfied with our workshops. This was rare, however, and when it did happen the group provided support and insight, giving us strength to learn from our less successful experiences.

In the beginning we thought we had to replicate Ora in order to succeed, but with time it became apparent that each of us could succeed with his or her own unique style, and that our joint work as co-facilitators gave our work an important depth and breadth. Workshop members found this fascinating, frequently commenting on how we worked together.

In looking back I think what was most amazing is how often Ora was right! She gave us concrete methods in FORMS that could be easily adopted. We did what we learned and it worked! Ora did not lecture, she modeled. She did not tell us what to do, she did it and we absorbed her model and took off from there. We then brought what we had learned and experienced to the teachers in our school workshops.

Chava Zohar, Center Staff

I had been a teacher for many years, elementary school in Israel and high school in England. I came back to Israel and studied educational counseling and I felt that teaching and counseling were things that I wanted to keep on doing. At the time I was around 42, and by coincidence (or not) a friend of mine who worked as a teaching assistant in the School of Education at the Hebrew University told me that there was an American woman teacher who wanted to set up a new center. She was looking for a group of teachers who would join her staff, and my friend thought it was just right for me. I took Ora's telephone number and I called. It was Friday, the course started on Monday, and she only accepted people after an interview. She said if I was working full time it would be impossible, but then it turned out that Monday was my free day.

Ora's course was different from anything I had ever experienced in all of my teacher education and training. It was different and interesting, the fulfillment of that something that I knew but did not know how to put into words. I felt like a vessel constantly filled with personal growth, and with counseling, teaching and group facilitation skills. I experienced a unique synergy created by the interactions among the different realms, all coming together to enable me to function more effectively. It was three-dimensional learning from the point of view of the learner. It was an incredible source of joy!

We met for a full day once a week for an entire year until we were prepared to go out into the field as workshop leaders. *Significance* was a central concept in all that we did. One of the first questions we always raised in a new group was, "Who was significant in your life? Which teacher, counselor? How was he/she significant?" We then worked through all the elements of *significance*. The participants brought to their classes what they experienced in the workshop and discovered how **they** could become significant in the lives of **their** students.

The work itself was very demanding and the traveling was difficult. All the staff members were teaching in the field as well which served to enhance our capabilities as workshop leaders. However, the Center staff meetings with Ora, which always began with HIGHLIGHTS and ECHOES, created a nurturing and supportive environment for all of us. We met on a regular basis throughout the school year, always analyzing, reflecting, and learning together in an environment characterized by openness, honesty, loyalty, wisdom, and friendship. For years, these meetings were the center of our lives.

Tamar Wolfin, School Principal

It was the beginning of the academic year, and I was taking my first steps in the Masters Degree program in Education in the maze of the

Mt. Scopus campus of the Hebrew University. I began the routine that accompanied me in the years to come: In the morning, I travelled to Kfar Blum, taught two classes, and hitched a ride to a bus going to Jerusalem. About four hours later, I got off at the bus station where my father was waiting for me in his car with the usual bag containing fruit in season that my mother had prepared for me. My father drove me to Mt. Scopus and I got there just in time for the 2:30 Sunday class.

One day I stood outside the elevator on the third floor and I began to peel a tangerine that was in the bag. Waiting next to me was a small woman with white hair, shining blue eyes and a trustworthy smile, and she said: "What a wonderful fragrance that tangerine has, it must also taste terrific." I immediately offered her a section of the fruit, but she refused politely with a smile.

The next morning I met my good friend from the Galilee who was already a veteran in the halls of the School of Education. I don't remember if she had any other advice, but her main recommendation was: Go study with Ora Zohar! Her course is probably already full, but you should try. And try I did. I got to the designated room, and discovered that Ora Zohar was the small woman with white hair, shining blue eyes and a trustworthy smile. I don't remember how I tried to convince her to let me into her class, but I remember her answer: "The course is full but I will accept you." And this was the beginning of a wonderful relationship.

The course dealt with the professional image of the principal. At the beginning of each lesson Ora would write the MENU, the lesson's outline, all written in English, all with clues, so that we could never know how each lesson would develop. But each time we concluded a heading, Ora would mark that we had been dealing with this issue. By the end of the lesson, we had a summary on the board, a summary built from the abstract clues with which the lesson had opened.

Looking back, a number of important things stand out for me about that course. The course tightly integrated the reading of research literature with reflecting on personal experiences and observing chosen principals. For the first time I was exposed to the tremendous amount of professional literature in the English language. I was in shock at the number of professional journals devoted entirely to the work of the school principal. At the same time, the papers we had to give in required us to not only read but also to reflect, to think and even to feel.

Later, when I became a principal, I had the privilege of attending the Principals' Center. Once again, I engaged in learning that combined research knowledge with inner reflection and learning from colleagues. The accepting atmosphere that prevailed in the course enabled all of us to be open to getting to know each other and to learning from our successes and difficulties. The integration of principals from the different sectors of Israeli society enriched the course greatly.

In this course too we opened each meeting with MENU, the same clues that turned into headings of an outline on the board. After the first two meetings, we already knew that the first clues dealt with who had come and who had not, and then we would share HIGHLIGHTS. It reminded me a bit of Sunday morning in kindergarten, when they begin with stories from the previous Shabbat. But when all is said and done, we were all kindergarten children who wanted to tell the teacher about what experiences we had since we last met. There were stories of a new grandchild, or overcoming a giant obstacle on the job, but there were also experiences of serious illness and loss. In contrast to kindergarten, here it was not only the teacher who listened, we all listened and enriched ourselves from the gifts we received from our colleagues.

I have a hard time pointing to the course's outcomes for me. I know that after every meeting I returned with something that made me a little bit different - different mostly in that I was more attuned to the staff that I managed. I initiated monthly meetings of "Roses and Thorns" in which 15 of the teachers and workers in the school got together, and each one would tell a little about himself. Then we would talk about the "thorns and roses" in the school. This idea sprouted from the seeds planted in the meetings of the Principals' Center. The workshop that we held for teachers in the school, which dealt with different pedagogical problems, succeeded in bringing many teachers to sit together and to openly share and discuss the things that were bothering them. I saw this as a great success.

I want to add another word about Ora's writing in English on the board in the classroom. It indeed was not obvious to me that a lecturer in the Hebrew University would write on the board in English. But in a discussion I once had with Ora she told me how she once took upon herself the role of *Mechanechet* for the 12th grade on condition that she could write in English rather than in Hebrew. One day an English teacher from the United States came to me, and displayed the qualities that could make her a good *Mechanechet*. Toward the end of her second trimester on the job, she told me that she wanted to stop being a *Mechanechet*. In talking with her, I realized that her main difficulty was with the Hebrew. I told her the story about Ora, and I told her that if it would help her she could write on the board in English. She also had a problem with the core topic of that year that required a lot of reading of Hebrew materials. The topic was related to Zionism and I suggested to her that she with her class could focus on getting to know a Jewish community in America, corresponding with high school students there, comparing their Jewish way of life to ours.

Leadership is a combination of power and control over materials and people, and fostering the right kind of relationships with people. Even an army commander who shouts : "After me!" and charges onward at the head of his troops, cannot be confident that they will follow him if during training he did not foster a supportive relationship, a relationship which at the crucial time will motivate them to charge after him. This is so much more the case in an educational institution, which indeed has a hierarchical structure, but not one based upon orders. Here it is especially critical to integrate a mastery of knowledge with the creation of a nurturing infrastructure with the staff, the students and the parents.

It is this integration that we learned in the Principals' Center.

Sara Wieder, Center Staff

Even before I completed my university studies, I taught in school as a class *Mechanechet*. It was only three years after I had received my teaching certificate from the university confirming my training as a teacher, and my teaching license from the Ministry of Education.

As a *Mechanechet* I had to manage a class and prepare a weekly class session on age-relevant topics drawn from current events. I had to develop a personal relationship with the girls, hold one-on-one conversations with them and plan parent meetings for reporting grades and discussing issues of interest to them.

I never received any training for the specific job of being a *Mechanechet*. Pedagogic studies at the university included one didactic seminar on the teaching profession. How did I do it? Somehow, I did and it went well.

I remember as a child I always wanted to be a teacher. My favorite game was playing Teacher, at first with dolls, and later with the names of my classmates, which I wrote on scraps of paper and organized in rows on the floor. Becoming a teacher was the realization of a dream. I suppose I acted out of intuition and perhaps an inborn talent. It goes without saying that the meetings with parents were preceded by days and nights of tension and anxiety!

After working as a teacher and *Mechanechet* for nearly 20 years, I heard about a course for *Mechanchim* offered by the National Center for Staff Development at the Hebrew University. I enrolled immediately. From the first moment I felt that this was exactly what I had been missing. Until taking the course, I had acted out of intuition, but frequently I felt lacking in confidence. In the course, I received the theoretical background essential to the role of the *Mechanech*, a role that required practicing and acquiring many interpersonal skills. I was exposed to Rogerian concepts such as empathy, acceptance, trust and sincerity. Finally, my intuition received academic backing.

We worked in small and large groups, and what we learned in the course did not stay in the realm of theory. We were asked to apply what we learned in the field, and then to come back and tell the group how it went.

I learned tools that were new to me that enhanced my ability to listen, to develop a relationship, to get to know someone new and to manage a constructive conversation. These new experiences provided insight into the essence and potential of the role of *Mechanechet*.

The tools and skills that I learned also affected my teaching in my subject specialty. I incorporated things such as working in small groups, writing a MENU with the lesson topics, varied SET INDUCTIONS and CLOSURES, giving more effective explanations and more.

My first parent meeting after starting the course was different from any I had previously planned. First of all, I was more confident to try new things. I no longer stood before the parents lecturing them all night about the importance of their relationship with their adolescent girls. Instead of talking, we did something.

I asked a few parents and their daughters to sit in small groups. The task was to describe the neighborhood in which they grew up, a topic that anyone could talk about easily. The girls heard various and assorted stories from their parents and from the parents of their friends and were encouraged to ask questions.

The pleasant noise that pervaded the room was different from anything I had ever experienced in a parent meeting. The spontaneous feedback gave me a wonderful feeling, as though new blood flowed through my role as a *Mechanechet*.

When I was a *Mechanechet* for the upper grades, I sought to change the structure of my weekly sessions with the class. Instead of always being with an entire class, sometimes we divided the class in two and I would work only with half of the students. This made it possible to sit in a circle (like in the workshop) in which everyone saw each other and many more girls had a chance to express themselves.

This new spirit reverberated in the teachers' lounge. Some of the teachers became infected by the new activities and the philosophy behind them. Some wanted to participate in the course in order to experience it for themselves.

Aviva Pinchuk, Center Staff

It was 1984 and this was to be my Maiden Voyage. My first workshop as a facilitator! And in England! I had studied with Ora for a year in her MA class in Hebrew University, and was a member of her RICH staff in creating a program for teaching Jewish values through English studies. I had been teaching for years, but a workshop leader? And in England? How could Ora trust me? I remember telling Ora the only reason I believed I could do it was because she told me!

And so, in February, with a small infant on my arms and a wonderful partner Rachel Karni at my side (and with Ora behind me!) the three of us boarded the EL AL flight to England. Rachel and I had met for many long hours to plan our several days with the staff of the Jewish Primary School just outside of London. On the plane, with the baby in my lap, we continued to discuss, review, and exchange ideas and fears (mainly mine!).

The next morning, we met with Michael Cohen, the then Head of the London Board of Jewish Education, who requested that special emphasis be placed on opening lines of communication between members of the staff and fostering a cooperative atmosphere among the teachers. Little did we realize then how significant this request would be!

On Sunday morning, a cheerful English nanny took my baby from my arms and reluctantly I left, holding on to Rachel for dear life, to be whisked away by a waiting car. Upon our arrival at the school, we set about the physical task of rearranging the chairs in a semi-circle for our participants. With MENU written on the board and our index cards in hands, we sat and waited for our clients to arrive.

And one by one they did, with not a smiling face among them. Was it the "English" in them, or do they hate us already? It took only moments to find out! We hardly said "Hello" when we were immediately met by outright resentment accompanied by furiously clacking knitting needles. They were all infuriated at being forced to give up a free day to participate in some unknown and somewhat mysterious course given by Israelis who had never stepped foot in the school before! It didn't help the situation when the Headmaster politely expressed **his** feelings of skepticism! My heart sank! I just wanted to flee! But I glanced at my partner Rachel who nodded and smiled and softly suggested we begin.

We opened the first session with great trepidation to say the least. Rachel began with great ease and confidence which encouraged me to calmly follow the plan we had worked so hard to formulate; Name Tags, Teachers in my Life, sharing pleasant memories and experiences, Miss A, Attending...The ice slowly seemed to melt and the sound of gnashing knitting needles seemed to dissipate. By the first break, we felt the entirely suspicious and even hostile feelings beginning to change to friendliness and eagerness. The Headmaster sat down next to us and told us the following: "You notice how all the teachers wrote their first names on their name tags and I wrote 'Mr. Morgan' (fictitious name) - because I feel very strongly that I can't give my first name to a stranger. I feel the use of a first name has to be earned. A person has to *deserve* using my first name. Well, I just want you to know that now I am changing my name tag to 'Louis'!"

With that encouragement, we pushed on to the more strenuous part of the program with much more confidence. The discussion and exercises on Goal Clarification provided the teachers from both the religious and secular staff the opportunity to explore and learn about each other's views on a crucial issue and in great depth. This activity created a new warmth and openness in the group. Although they were in a hurry to get home, most of the teachers came over to us to say "Thank you" and the Headmaster remarked that this was the first opportunity the teachers had for "socializing, talking, and discussing."

Over the next two days, we were witness to serious and focused discussions among the staff members in a friendly and accepting environment. During the last activity we call LOOKING AHEAD, one of the teachers remarked, "Why don't we have meetings like this during the year?" Three teachers immediately volunteered to plan and chair the first such meeting, which was to take place a few weeks after our departure. We offered our help if necessary and they promised to send us a report of their first meeting. The Headmaster presented each of us with a gift and warm expressions of gratitude. We left encouraged and motivated to continue working with teachers wherever they might be!

Training under Ora and working with an experienced and sensitive partner is what made my maiden voyage a successful sail. There were times of smooth sailing and then moments of choppy seas when the feeling of inadequacy and inexperience crept aboard. Rachel was always there with her lifesaver! From her I learned detailed planning is not the only factor for success. I learned that at times you have to put down the index cards for a while and be sensitive to the needs of the group. I returned to Israel with a happy baby and a suitcase filled with a sense of learning and accomplishment, newly gained confidence, appreciation of my partner's personal and professional qualities, and deep gratitude to Ora for having given me this opportunity.

I felt ready for my next voyage!

A thought provoking P.S. – Just before our departure for Israel, we had an informal meeting with the then Chief Rabbi of Great Britain, Lord Jakobovits, who took great interest in our work. After hearing our report he asked, "Can this program be effective with Rabbis?" Our immediate response – "Absolutely!"

Rachel Karni, Center Staff

I go a long way back with Ora, to the period when she worked at Bar Ilan University. As an English teacher, I participated and presented at the Bar Ilan in-service summer courses for English teachers that she organized. Not long afterward, I was privileged to be in the first group at the Hebrew University whose participants Ora meticulously trained to facilitate workshops.

The innovations that Ora introduced were unique and left a permanent impact on those who experienced them. The focus was on how to get people in school systems to function at a higher level, thus benefitting the learners. This could not be accomplished through structural changes alone; it required intensive contact with people and building relationships.

In one specific case, that of workshops that took place as part of a course for English department chairmen, I was in a position to observe the long-term effect of the workshop on the participants and on their subsequent functioning in their professions. Shortly after the Center began its work, the Ministry of Education sponsored a course for Heads of English departments that took place at the Hebrew University, meeting once a week for six hours. A bi-weekly three-hour workshop led by Chava Greenberg and myself was a major component of this course. Many of the participants in this group became leading figures in English education over the next twenty years. Three years later, Chava and I led a similar group at Bar Ilan University. In the years since, I have been able to follow the impact of these workshops on the participants: on the in-service courses they themselves organized, on the textbooks they wrote, and on their relationships with the teachers they supervised or mentored. Years later, one of the participants told me that she had spent many years in academic study, but the Center workshop "was the best course she had ever taken at a university." Over the years, I have heard this repeatedly.

Because of my affiliation with the Center, I remained a teacher of English for 38 years. My work with the Center gave me a completely new outlook on my profession, and provided many challenges through which I grew personally and professionally.

Iri Kessel, Principal and Center Staff

I first met Ora in 1986. Those were very enriching years – both those in which I learned and those in which I was on the staff.

Ora fashioned three truths:

- The central role of the principal is fashioning the school – its culture, the place of the teacher, and modes of learning.

- Every person strives to develop.

- Every person can develop in a systematic way.

The principal has a significant role in enabling development, in enabling expression. The principal needs to chart the course, to provide people with a place to breathe, to do, and to create.

All the workshops at the Principals' Center integrated three components:

- academic knowledge, research, up-to-date articles,

- facilitation designed to connect between day-to-day realities and academic knowledge,

- use of the experience of people in the field.

The group consisted of very diverse participants, and their varied experiences were enriching and motivating.

In the Principals' Center the setting was very significant – three-day sessions, six sessions for each cohort. There was a sense of togetherness, a peaceful environment, a bridge over troubled waters. Principals left behind the noise, the commotion, the intensive hyperactive doing, for a retreat of peacefulness and quiet reflection.

It was at the Principals' Center that I started to write a diary at the end of every day. It helps me to sharpen my thoughts, to define, to focus. It is a tool for monitoring how things are developing.

HIGHLIGHTS is an amazing activity – to think about something positive. The mere act of talking about the positive changes the mood. Slowly we discovered that people want to highlight the positive.

One of the activities I initiated as a result of my participation in the Principals' Center was "10 minutes on...". Each week on a different day, we extended the hour of the pastoral care lesson for teachers only. We made sure to prepare tea or coffee in advance, and we invited each teacher to talk for 10 minutes about something he or she did. This provided a stage for all members of the staff, especially for people who did not usually have the confidence to speak.

From the workshops at the Principals' Center I have learned to enable people to think about challenges and how they can rise to meet them. What more can you do to improve things for both you and the organization? People constantly need to be helped to see the challenges, to expand the boundaries of their role, to look for more challenges. I like to offer people a field that they can develop, not necessarily in a managerial position.

I have learned to recognize the power of placing emphasis on giving positive reinforcement to teachers. I say thank you for everything. If someone does something good, I immediately give positive feedback – an e-mail, praise in a staff meeting. For the person it means so much. We need to encourage people to develop, to let them feel that their contribution is recognized. Afterwards it also makes it possible to give criticism when necessary. It is very hard to tell people/teachers that they made a mistake. It is hard to receive criticism. When someone knows that you value him or her it is still hard, but it makes it easier.

Susan Haber, Center Staff

As a beginning teacher of high school French in Brooklyn, New York, I pictured my role as that of a drill sergeant. I had to be fully in charge, conduct the class at a fast pace and drill the basic elements of my subject, e.g. vocabulary, grammar, sentence patterns. I had some small success, probably because I would be giving out the marks at the end of the year. However, I found myself spending a lot of time trying to get the pupils to pay attention and cooperate. The enthusiasm that I tried to exude and the rigid, tense tempo of the lesson I tried to orchestrate did not do much to improve the situation.

When I joined Ora's workshop leaders' group at Hebrew University about ten years later, my ideas about teaching had not changed much. In fact, I remember that, early in the course, as a discussion leader in a micro-teaching exercise, I very determinedly and unsuccessfully tried to convince an unwilling group of teachers to accept my point of view.

That year Ora presented ideas and modeled a kind of teaching that would completely change my teaching style. In particular, the idea of changing the teacher's role from "expert" to the "facilitator of learning" became my guiding principle. Subsequently, in my work with pupils, mainly at the lower levels in English, I found Ora's training to be invaluable. I tried to create an atmosphere of openness, acceptance, and encouragement where pupils would be free to do their best. At the end of each year when pupils gave their evaluation of the course, they invariably expressed appreciation for the atmosphere that allowed them to succeed. For this success, I owe a great debt to Ora Zohar.

Epilogue: Back to Mr. Goldberg

Today, reflecting on the development of the Center's work, I marvel at the link to Mr. Goldberg's comment of long, long ago: "Well, you see, in this school we teach children, and Ora knows children very well." This has been our basic message to teachers and the foundation of our ability to offer school-based staff development rather than subject-centered groups. This has allowed us to invite the entire teaching staff of a community to work together, across age levels or curriculum restraints.

Truly, this approach was the heart of our success in Jewish schools abroad where there is often a great divide between the Jewish studies and General studies staff. In some schools, there are literally different areas in the faculty lunch room for staff of different subjects. Often, this reality limited the discussion and participation of much of the staff concerning relevant school issues, such as goal setting, discipline policy, parent-school partnerships, character development, gender related issues, professional policy. Thus, for a community wishing to invest in professional staff development in the fullest framework possible, our workshops were very attractive. There was no possible resentment on the part of one staff about the resources poured into another.

In the very first group workshop I gave abroad, where for financial reasons I was exploring the possibility of translating the one-to-one model of the Clinic into a group model, I learned of the Great Divide. The principal had suggested I work with ten department chairpersons in the school on issues of supervision, classroom observation and teaching improvement. At the end of an intensive week of training, several of the participants came to thank me, saying, "We've been on staff in this school for ten, twelve or more years, and have never even spoken to each other! He teaches Bible, while I teach math, or history and we barely knew each other's names! After these few days of studying, sharing and thinking together, at last we feel that we teach in the same school! Thank you, thank you!" By chance or not, that school was located within walking distance of Mr. Goldberg's Hebrew school in Brooklyn.

That message has resounded in schools in Israel, England, Australia, the United States, South Africa and Mexico. "Thank you," they say. "Thank you for reminding us that we all teach the same children in the same school. Thank you for reminding us that we have more in common than not; that we all teach children, and not subject matter alone."

Across the world and across a professional lifetime, I also say, "Thank you, Mr. Goldberg."

Ora Zohar

Bibliography

Allen, Dwight. *Microteaching.* Reading, Mass.: Addison-Wesley Publishing, 1969.

Aronson, Elliot, & Patnoe, Shelly. *Cooperation in the Classroom: The Jigsaw Method* (3rd ed.). London: Pinter & Martin, 2011.

Barth, Roland. *Improving Schools from Within: Teachers, Parents, and Principals can Make the Difference.* San Francisco: Jossey-Bass, 1990.

Deal, Terrence E. "The Symbolism of Effective Schools." *Elementary School Journal* (1978) 5:601–20.

Deal, Terrence E. and Peterson, Kent D. *The Leadership Paradox: Balancing Logic and Artistry in Schools.* San Francisco: Jossey-Bass, 1994.

Dewey, John. *Democracy and Education, An Introduction to the Philosophy of Education.* New York: Macmillan, 1916.

Erikson, Erik H., *Childhood and Society.* New York: W.W. Norton and Co., 1950.

Frankl, Victor E. *Man's Search for Meaning.* Boston: Beacon Press, 1959.

Maslow, Abraham H. *Motivation and Personality.* New York: Harper & Row, 1954.

Maslow, Abraham H. *Toward A Psychology of Being.* New York: Van Nostrand, 1962.

Pedersen, Eigil and Faucher, Therese A. and Eaton, William W. "A New Perspective on the Effects of First-Grade Teachers on Children's Subsequent Adult Status." *Harvard Educational Review* 48 (1978): 1–31.

Rogers, Carl. *On Becoming a Person.* Boston: Houghton Mifflin, 1961.

Rogers, Carl. *Freedom to Learn for the 80s.* Columbus, Ohio: C.E. Merril Pub. Co., 1983.

Schön, Donald A. *The Reflective Practitioner, How Professionals Think in Action*. Boston: Arena Publishing Co., 1983.

Schon, Donald A. *Educating the Reflective Practitioner: Toward a New Design for Teaching and Learning in the Professions*. San Francisco: Jossey Bass, 1987.

Sergiovanni, Thomas J., ed. *Supervision of Teaching.* Alexandria, Virginia: Association for Supervision and Curriculum Development (ASCD) Yearbook, 1982.

Sergiovanni, Thomas J. and Starratt, Robert. *Supervision: Human Perspectives.* New York: McGraw-Hill, 1983.

Sergiovanni, Thomas J. *Leadership for the Schoolhouse: How is it Different? Why is it Important?* San Francisco, Calif.: Jossey-Bass, 1996.

Sergiovanni, Thomas J. *The Principalship, A Reflective Practice Perspective,* 6th ed. Boston: Pearson, 2009.

Glossary

ATTENDING – Listening wholeheartedly and compassionately to the other. ATTENDING is a conscious and purposeful activity that expresses itself through body language. Dwight Allen broke down ATTENDING into its different parts and these were practiced systematically in every workshop.

BACKSTAGE – A FORM that consists of a review and analysis of the step-by-step process of workshop hours spent together. We invite participants to go back to the MENU and with its help to recall with us what had taken place in the workshop. Looking at each activity, we share with them what we had planned and why, what options we faced as the process progressed, and why we made particular choices.

CLOSURES – A structured individual and group opportunity to reflect upon the year coming to a close, relating to all aspects of job performance.

CODES – A shorthand device based on acronyms that provides facilitators with a kind of checklist for navigating their way through complex situations.

CREASIS – A CODE used to help in the facilitation of role plays. It is an acronym for Comprehension, Creativity, Review, Rehearsal, Empathy, Awareness, Set Induction, Introspection, Imagination, and Stretching.

ECHOES - Reports of applying an aspect of the workshop in the classroom or school life since the last meeting. Participants are asked to take one or two workshop activities into their own classroom and to relate the experience to us. Eventually, in every group, participants begin to share their ECHOES with the group.

FIVE –TIONS (pronounced *shuns*) – A code used by staff to plan for difficult meetings in which they anticipate confrontation or hostility. The FIVE –TIONS include Validation, Clarification, Consideration, Cooperation, and Coordination.

FORMS – Structured educational processes developed in the Center that create supportive learning environments. They include simple techniques, concepts or activities that are easily applicable to nearly every workshop setting.

HIGHLIGHTS - Sharing a positive personal experience or event with workshop participants. HIGHLIGHTS is critical because it invites participants to pay attention to the things in life and at work for which they are grateful, and encourages them to see the group as a place to share them.

MARCHING AND DANCING – Two different ways to approach classroom learning. In MARCHING, the emphasis is on keeping in step as everyone moves in the same direction at the same pace. DANCING, in contrast, is much more varied – one may dance solo or in pairs, in ballroom dancing, or in wild groups of folk dancing, accompanied by song or instrument. In DANCING with the material, we review, recall, reflect; alone, in pairs, in a large group; as homework or as a group project.

MEMBER – In this FORM a different member of the group is invited each session to talk to the group for seven to ten minutes about his past, schooling, and choice of profession. He may choose what to relate and what to omit. If he is willing to take questions from the group, the activity lasts approximately 15 minutes. Secrecy is an important element of this FORM. Only the MEMBER-of-the-day knows who has been chosen.

MENU - A clear statement of the planned program that is written on the board prior to the beginning of a class or workshop.

MISS A – An elementary school teacher in Canada in the 1950's and 1960's who was found by a McGill professor of education to have had an extraordinary positive impact upon her students' lifelong success. A former pupil summarized her secret for success: "How did she teach? With a lot of love!" Miss A became a CODE in workshops for teachers who made a difference in their students' lives.

MISS DARCY – A poem written by Florence Wallach Freed recalling her experience of her first grade teacher. The poem is used as a set induction to arouse memories of school traumas, and to consider how to prevent the reoccurrence of such traumas today. "Darcy Dimensions" became a code word.

MISSING – When taking attendance in every session, in a far upper corner of the board, MISSING is written, and a list is made of anyone not present. MISSING gives a message that someone notices whether we are present or not, and that if we are not there we are missed.

OUR CLIENT – A snapshot showing a group of small children, six or seven years old, seated in rows in a classroom. It was taken from the first page of a local newspaper under the heading "The First Day of School." The children's faces exhibit fear, tension, and anxiety. The picture is used as a SET INDUCTION for a unit called "Meet Our Client."

SET INDUCTION - A SET INDUCTION sets the stage for learning about a new issue or theme. It could be a song, an anecdote, an item of jewelry or clothing, a toy, tool, stuffed animal, food, concept, quote.... A SET INDUCTION is like the music being played as we enter the theater. It sets the emotional tone of the play that we are about to see; it prepares us for the mood even as we settle into our seats; it is with us as the curtain goes up.

SHRT – Systematic Human Relationship Training exercises are activities designed to generate acceptance, understanding, and empathy among the participants or members of a group.

SPECIAL – A CODE used by staff to aid in planning and reviewing workshop sessions. It is an acronym for Social, Sharing, Secret, Personal, Experiential, Empathy, Communication, Connectedness, Introspection, Attending, Awareness, Learning

About the Author

Dr. Ora Zohar was born in Jerusalem and educated in the U.S. She earned her doctorate in Staff Development at the University of Massachusetts in Amherst, and went on to found the National Center for Teaching Improvement and Staff Development at the Hebrew University in Jerusalem. She has been involved in training educators for over six decades in many places around the world. She currently resides in Jerusalem with her husband, children and many grandchildren and great-grandchildren.

With:

Aviva Pinchuk, a native of Jerusalem, holds a degree in Education and Teaching English as a Foreign Language. She taught for more than 25 years abroad and in secular high schools in Jerusalem while serving as a staff member of the National Center for Teaching Improvement and Staff Development, and was a member of the RICH staff for English curriculum development.

Sara Wieder has a Masters degree in Education and History from the Hebrew University in Jerusalem. She served as a teacher in a religious high school in Jerusalem and in the Israel Ministry of Education as supervisor for the teaching of history in religious schools. As a member of staff at the National Center for Teaching Improvement and Staff Development, Sara facilitated staff development workshops for teachers in both elementary schools and high schools, and worked with a wide range of principals in the Principals' Center at the Hebrew University.

Chava Zohar, a native of Jerusalem, is a graduate of the David Yellin College for Teacher Training, the Hebrew University School of Education, and the program in Educational Counseling at the University of Michigan. As a member of staff at the National Center for Teaching Improvement and Staff Development, she facilitated workshops in the Jewish, Druze, and Arab sectors in Israel, and trained teachers and principals in Europe, Canada, and South Africa.

Edited by:

Israel Sykes, born and raised in Baltimore, has lived and worked in Israel for over thirty years as a social entrepreneur, organizational consultant, family therapist and action researcher. He lives in Jerusalem with his wife Naava and four children, all fortunate to have grown up with Ora Zohar as their grandmother.

www.ingramcontent.com/pod-product-compliance
Lightning Source LLC
Chambersburg PA
CBHW052042090426
42739CB00010B/2011